INFORMATION TECHNOLOGY
A Revolutionary Change

INFORMATION TECHNOLOGY
A Revolutionary Change
(In 9 Volumes)

Volume 7
(Networking and Educating Multiculturally)

Editor
RAMESH CHANDRA
Vice-Chancellor, Bundelkhand University, Jhansi (U.P.)

KALPAZ PUBLICATIONS
DELHI–110052

INFORMATION TECHNOLOGY: A REVOLUTIONARY CHANGE

(Information Technology)

Rs. 8000 (Set)
Rs. 900 (Each Volume)

ISBN: 81-7835-201-X (Set)
ISBN: 81-7835-226-5 (Vol. 7)

Published in 2003 in India by
Kalpaz Publications
C–30, Satyawati Nagar
Delhi–110052
E-mail: kalpaz@hotmail.com

Laser Typesetting at: Varsha Graphics, Delhi
Printed at: Mehra Offset Printers, New Delhi

Contents

Preface

The information and communication technologies (ICTS) provides new resources and material for expanding education. The interactive dimension of new multimedia technology can potentially involve students more integrally into historical research and enhance moral understanding, thus providing powerful pedagogical tools to teach tolerance and promote a multicultural and an anti-racist curricula. A mechanistic and all-too-common reductive abstraction of teaching from human experience and multidisciplinary perspectives can be overcome in part through the use of new multimedia as teaching devices.

The net-based education can help access to lived experience, as well as dramatize and concretize basic historical facts and knowledge. Many current criticisms of the role of computer and multimedia technology in the school stem from an inability to grasp the nature and importance of computer literacy and to understand how new technologies can help revitalize education. This failure to embrace new technologies as a teaching device has been preceded by an uneven and never adequate use of film and television material in the classroom.

The use of the most advanced technologies for educational purposes, is beneficial to showing how new technologies can advance and revitalize education for today's student. Creative use of new technologies, of course, depends on those who implement them and how they are deployed. Effective use is nurtured by the convictions and sustained efforts that must accompany projects embodying imaginative teaching designs and programs to further multicultural education and teaching of events, otherwise hard to grasp. A democratic and multicultural reconstruction of education thus requires the commitment and critical intelligence-as well as hard work!-of teachers, in conjunction with the students who so desperately need these kinds of resources to truly learn about the world, and hence themselves and their place in it.

Many educators and critics thus denounce out-of-hand new computer technologies rather than embarking on serious studies of how such tools can be used to enhance education. In a similar vein, criticisms are also proliferating concerning student propensities toward employing the computer, Internet, and the World Wide Web to plagiarize and cheat on term paper assignments, rather than seriously investigating the ways that computers and multimedia could be productively used to advance research and education. Such criticism obscures the real kinds of epistemological and behavioral shifts that an expanding computer and media culture are producing and the need to develop literacies and pedagogies to make use of these technologies for educational purposes.

Editor

1

Networking in Higher Education

Notwithstanding the financial challenges faced by both educational institutions themselves and their suppliers over the last five years, the concept of higher education as a business sector has become firmly established. Indeed, one example of this is University Business's listing of 280 higher education consultants. The range of specialist services offered, including financial aid, marketing, minority issues, technology, management, book shop services, libraries and fund-raising, indicates the degree of 'unbundling' that has occurred within the education sector. A further indicator is that resistance to the business lexicon, has almost evaporated: university committees routinely debate 'product', 'brand', and 'strategic positioning' without irony or inverted commas. Much has been argued in relation to the potential of universities to supplement their income, and work with industry and business through tailoring of programmes and links with corporate training units. Certainly many institutions in the US, as elsewhere, are seeking such business with business.

> However, according to a Corporate Universities Xchange survey, universities have not become a major beneficiary of corporate university outsourcing. Rather, 37 per cent of contracts are with training vendors, which are more 'business-savvy' than universities, and more flexible; only 16 per cent of contracts involve universities.

This should not be surprising: not because universities are reluctant to engage with industry in providing short courses or degree programmes, indeed the evidence is to the contrary, but because so much of the company training market (estimated variously at US$ 66 billion to a low US$ 26.7 billion is simply new product training or low level IT upgrade training. Urdan and Huggen in fact that two-thirds of outsourced training in 1999 was in IT, and of this, only a quarter used technology-based delivery. A full 75 per cent of corporate training was still instructor-led in late 1999. The level of such training might be deduced from the largest expanding area of the for-profit sector: 28 per cent of two-year college programmes are now delivered in the for-profits, according to the Education Commission of the States.

One might observe that IT skills are more properly the preserve of the VET sector, andsome training is company specific. Online or video-delivered programmes arenevertheless a boon in such training, since they can reduce the costs of attendance atprogrammes, typically two-thirds of total training costs. Strategically-governed universities seeking to find alternate revenue sources via vocationally-oriented programmes are increasingly likely to focus on a niche market strategy, 'a selected vertical market', where the institution has a clear advantage through the reputation of a particular course, because so many for-profit providers have entered the market in generic products in narrow fields like business and IT, which were predicted to be the profitable areas.

The University of Pennsylvania's World Campus, for example, has decided on a select range of online programmes, based on its reputation in specific areas such as Adult Education, and Logistics; it also specialises in shorter Certificate level courses, in recognition of the greater attraction of brief commitments in continuing professional education. Carnegie Mellon has leveraged its reputation in electronic commerce. In Australia, some universities have already implemented this strategy, as the University of NSW has capitalised on its reputation in professional tax education and training, or as QUT's Faculty of Information Technology leverages its partnership with Cisco through the Cisco Networking Academy Program. Obviously, the advantage of the niche course approach is that it concentrates resources and staff, rather than dissipates energy and financial resources across the institution, which is the unfortunate effect of many Australian universities' 'flexible delivery' decisions. Alternately, a university could focus on a particular segment of the market, as UoP has captured the working adult with no pretensions to accessing an elite institution, and with the capacity to pay more for convenience. This appears to be an element of the strategy adopted by the Global University Alliance consortium in relation to its online MBA programme.

We observed that a number of e-learning portals has been established to direct potential students to universities on a commission basis. Dedicated commercial sites such as HungryMinds, Edupoint and Headlight have not prospered, partly because so many public sites now list distance education opportunities, and because, as we noted in relation to Western Governors, potential students can go directly to a provider institution's site. In the main, universities have now abandoned the use of portals to advertise and bring students to the institution; Penn State dropped Hungry Minds and other e-learning portals which link to enrolment information, because 'eyeballs do not convert to tuition dollars'. Instead, Penn State uses professional magazines and targeted advertising to professional groups. Often institutions prefer to offer a free introductory module of a programme, which does not attract a fee unless the student wishes to convert it to credit.

One potentially more promising model is the Monster.com launch of MonsterLearning. TMP Worldwide, formerly recruitment company Morgan and Banks, has developed an online resume service which now claims 74.5 millionusers, and a search tool which allows users to access a database of 15 000 awardand non-award online and class-based subjects in Accounting, It and Finance. MonsterLearning will develop a skills gap analysis feature that will then recommend subjects and programmes from its list to resume posters. Education providers pay membership fees of US$2000 to US$50 000 annually to advertise their wares. However, whether such a directive tool will convert into enrolments is a moot point. In any event, universities and colleges may be forced by such activities into spending even more on marketing, although the success of such marketing is not guaranteed, as the Hungry Minds experience demonstrates. Other business opportunities in educational services may emerge. E-learning infrastructure and testing companies have been encouraged by shifts in educational policy within the US and other countries towards a greater degree of accountability from individual institutions in terms of learning outcomes.

In many US states and school districts, mandated standardised testing at specified grade levels determines funding for schools. A national trend to standardised exit tests across higher education, calling into question the autonomy of current accreditation procedures, and the quality guarantees given by individual universities and departments. Since most of these tests are conducted by private companies, such as CTB/McGraw-Hill, profitability in this sector is expected to soar, according to most education analysts, with concomitant effects on the profitability of software companies supporting the data processing of results. There are clear synergies for publishers acquiring test instruments in textbook and online resource sales, as well as professional development programmes for teachers. For example, Harcourt, a subsidiary of Reed Elsevier plc, publishes the Stanford Achievement Test, the most widely used norm-referenced test in the US, at 15 million students annually. Harcourt has now purchased Classroom Connect, a K-12 provider of both online curriculum materials and professional development for teachers, demonstrating publishers' clear determination to cover the testing, publishing and continuing professional development education market.

> Although it is to be expected that moves to standardised testing will be resisted in the higher education sector, the pressure of high numbers in a mass education system has already increased the use of computerised assessment items, and the difficulties associated with constructing valid and complex tests in markable digital form, would

suggest that such testing might become more centralised and 'corporatised' through outsourcing to specialist firms.

Combined with corporate universities' activities in workplace education and training, and the trend already noted here for students to prefer short or non-award subjects directly relevant to their work, such activities might suggest that traditional universities may face difficulty in expanding continuing professional education enrolments.

Other business opportunities have emerged through the certification movement, which has strengthened the positions of testing companies, which can offer secure test premises and systems. National Computer Systems, for example, established Virtual Universities Enterprises Authorised Testing Centres, 700 in all, providing for certificated testing for Microsoft, IBM and Novell, among other clients. Companies specialising in test preparation for certification examinations have also spawned, an example being the National Pharmacy Technician Certification, and the public float of the Princeton Review, a test preparation company enrolling 100 000 students annually. The latter has not captured market favour since its June float. It too has diversified from its preparation role: in launching Review.com, it offers a portal to information on financial aid, along with links to its commercial activities. This diversification of business activity within such firms is an indication of the confusion regarding business models that many in the industry are suffering in consequence of the slamming of the door on the equity injections which sustained e-learning service companies until April 2000. Amongst the non-profit education service sector firms, the trend, as in non-profit universities, has been to the establishment of for-profit subsidiaries.

Educational Testing Service, which administers the SAT and Advanced Placement tests, has invested in College Board, which hopes to market recruitment and financial aid information services to students applying for tests via a revamped portal and organising software. Even the philanthropic Sloan Foundation, which had sponsored an online consortium of over 80 colleges and universities (including MIT) offering web-based programmes, tried to market these programmes through the for-profit EduPoint, an aggregator of courses for the corporate market. The latter has not however, been successful. The 'shake-out' predicted by Microsoft's Joe Powell in the BBE, was exacerbated not only by the effect of market forces expected in any emergent industry with excessive supply, but also by the 'irrational exuberance' associated with an over-supply of capital, and the hype of many analysts' predictions of profit in a fledgling industry.

> A strategy among the survivors is cross-ownership, substantial investment and partnerships, such as that between publisher Pearsons and netLibrary, to create (and on-license) digital versions of Pearsons' texts. Pearsons has itself customised the Blackboard platform for its CourseCompass digitised text venture. Yet, as analysts such as Urdan and Huggen point out, 'currently all the players appear to be partnering with each other', and 'part of the value of a partnership is its exclusivity'. The same observation could be made of the multiple partnerships entered into by universities themselves: Columbia's major venture in Fathom competes with its interest in Cardean University, for example, and it is difficult to see how both investments are sustainable.

Most programming in for-profit, corporate and online providers was in the areas of IT, and Business, and that 'soft skills' were difficult to translate into the online platform. Nevertheless, Urdan and Huggen, among others, consider that soft skills training will migrate increasingly to an internet environment. There is little indication of this at present. Two contra-indications in the business of education are the emergence of open source code for many of the functions currently offered by commercial vendors, and the slow emergence of resource banks of teaching materials online. The North Carolina State University My-Library Portal Project allows script downloads in PERL, which may reduce sales as more institutions note the business failures of their suppliers, and either choose to develop their own systems, or choose major suppliers.

The Java Special Interest Group, JA-SIG, a research consortium of major universities, develops and shares applications for use in portals amongst the group, but may distribute its software more widely. Of great interest is MIT's decision to develop OpenCourseWare, a course development and content project to place 2000 subject resources and curricula, including assignment topics, on the web. MIT will make these freely available for use or adaptation. The cost of the project is estimated at US$100 million over 10 years, with some funding coming from private sources. The decision was announced as an altruistic initiative designed to counter commercial exploitation of the internet, in which MIT had a more than passing interest as a result of its research and application in online technologies. Although staff had been widely consulted via a long sequence of seminars on the issues involved, not all staff are convinced of the value of placing materials online, and copyright issues have risen as a concern. However, it is clear that since this is a university-wide initiative, and staff will be employed to assist academics to place their materials online, 'co-ownership' principles will be adopted.

The issue is less pertinent at MIT than elsewhere because there is no intention to profit commercially from the venture. Participation is voluntary, but all staff would be expected to progressively move their materials online, and the ten-year time frame seems likely to make this feasible. Analysts' reactions to this venture are intriguing: Newman (2001) doubts it will dent the commercial content providers' business, since simply posting content does not ensure learning, nor develop the necessary learning community needed to ensure student retention and motivation. Such observations are in distinct contrast to their enthusiasm for stand-alone generic vendor products. A further project, the Open Knowledge Initiative, is being led from MIT, in a consortium of Stanford, Harvard, Wisconsin, Pennsylvania, North Carolina, Dartmouth, and IMS, as well as Cambridge. The intention is to develop a learner management system in open source code for Internet. Interestingly, OpenCourseWare is not committed to using the OKI platform.

The MIT initiative has not prevented MIT from entering other for-profit online ventures, such as its arrangement with the PBS Business Channel to offer Certificates of Completion (not award programmes) in web-based subjects, Internet Commerce and Supply Chain. The subjects consist of two hours per week of streamed video or video satellite delivery, with an additional four hours per week of assignments, over six weeks. Student support is built in, with email discussion groups and telephone tutoring. At the University of Maryland, the Faculty Online Technology Training Consortium has assembled a professional development programme to prepare staff to use online technologies, and to share their teaching and learning materials. The course is freely available.

The organisation is growing rapidly after a slow start. As the responses to AAHESGIT's proposed Open Source Professional Development Environment make clear (AAHESGIT-121: 3/10/01), the financial and cultural challenges posed by open source shared resources are immense. At the same time, 'the spirit of the internet' as a vehicle for freely shared research has been asserted by university and public agency research communities. For physicists, mathematicians and computer scientists, the Los Alamos E-Print Archive has long operated as a free posting and retrieval service for original papers, many already submitted to peer-reviewed journals. Those associated with the database note its altruistic motive, since two-thirds of its 'visits' are from outside the US, and it is considered an essential resource for developing country scientists, where the costs of journals are increasingly prohibitive.

The founder of the archive intends to take the database to Cornell University, and to expand its offerings into other disciplines: Paul Ginsbarg believes that ultimately, the web could function as a first source, 'raw data' archive, freely available, while research articles wind their way through peer review and commercial journal publication. Many academics are now attempting to challenge the commercial publishers' domination of discipline knowledge and the soaring prices of academic journals. One such challenge is an attempt to begin a series of low cost online social science journals which pay for peer review, but which also remain cheap for subscribers by virtue of their online-only distribution costs and CHE online edition, March 9, 2001.

Another is the launch of SPARC, Scholarly Publishing and Academic Resources Coalition, which distributes science journals to 180 libraries in four continents. SPARC began BioOne, a network which will publish 40 journals online. A UK initiative, the Public Library of Science, supported by scientists from 170 countries, declared a boycott of major publishers, especially Elsevier, starting September 1. Most publishers have refused the scientists' demands for free online access to full text journals within six months of hard copy publication. It will be interesting to observe the outcome.

> It is apparent that the imperatives of the business of education collide with the ethos of both the academic and the internet worlds; there is unlikely to be any short-term resolution to the struggle for academic principles of openness and speedy distribution of research and teaching resources, while so many in higher education see the potential for individual gain in their university-based endeavours.

What has become clearer since the 2000, is that quality online education programmes from 'brand name' institutions have not delivered cost savings at the institutional level. Staffing costs have increased, reflecting both the longer time teaching staff must spend in interactive teaching, and the expense of technical and administrative support systems. The University of Florida's online MBA students pay three times the on-campus tuition fee, reflecting higher delivery costs and a more intensive and interactive teaching strategy. Both Keller Graduate School of Management and UoP, as noted in the 2000, charge more for their online courses, although the profit margin is greater for their online programme.

> Clearly, universities seeking to profit from online programmes face difficult choices in terms of pricing, and pedagogic approach. The mass distribution model of simply putting resources online has not been adopted by reputable institutions, or has not

> been viable where it was used, and the teaching 'service' in the online environment remains the most expensive budget element. This is so even where for-profit organisations, such as UoPOnline and Keller, utilise casual tutor labour.

Some institutions, an extension of their student cohort as a result on online offerings, but numbers remain small. The University of Florida, for example, has a mere 40 students per year in its online MBA, while UMUCOnline 's MBA has 30 students.

> One pertinent observation on the education business supports the warning of Jim Mingle of SHEEO in the BBE, in his concern about market forces pressing on education provision: 'the market won't support research, except in the most applied way, the arts and sciences, small institutions, programmes and fields, and students who can't pay full price - low income students'. Sir James Watson, VC of Brighton University in the UK, in a paper on funding for the education sector, noted that in London particularly, 'universities with the most progressive social missions are beginning to look like market failures' as a consequence of low enrolments and students choosing 'better brands', as all institutions seek to increase enrolments in a declining market. A number of UK progressive universities whose focus has traditionally been on marginalised students, comprehensive programme offerings, supplementary learner support, and strong teaching profiles, are facing mergers or closure.

The Borderlessness of Education

The conditions that impelled predictions of a borderless education industry in the late 1990s have increased in intensity since our 2000 publication, notwithstanding the failures of many online eduction ventures. Twigg, that 63 per cent of all colleges and universities in the US are already engaged in distance and distributed eduction at some level, with another 31 per cent planning to do so. 'National' companies have become international in focus; international organisations such as the World Bank and the OECD have argued the case for online education and training as a developmental responsibility of donor countries; internet connections have increased even in developing economies; 'globalisation' has become a topical issue of concern to citizens and politicians as well as economists. Small scale examples of internationalisation by universities abound, although these are usually at the level of physical programmes: staff and student exchanges; curriculum 'export' to a partner institution; and physical 'branch campuses' as with Cornell's planned medical campus in Qatar at that country's expense; and Sylvan's purchase of several overseas institutions.

The National University of Singapore plans a 'reverse' move to the usual pattern: the establishment of a college specialising in IT in California's Silicon Valley, while the Indian government reportedly has committed US$14 million to MIT to co-develop Media Lab Asia, to develop technologies of benefit to the rural poor. Other ventures are in embryonic, even test-tube stage: Universitas21, as noted, has achieved its student and staff mobility aims, but remains in development mode; UoPOnline remains largely a continental American operation. However, higher education has far to go before it can boast of being a global industry, and attaining the level of internationalisation achieved by top US companies, which glean 30-65 percent of their revenues offshore. Yet there is no shortage of contenders for global education provision, with one of the most ambitious being the UK's proposed e-university. Further, the US university sector remains in the early stages of understanding globalising influences on higher education, as the Ford Foundation's 2000 sponsorship of The Futures Project: Policy for Higher Education in a Changing World at Brown University demonstrates. A booming economy, a large population, and low unemployment made inward-looking policies and complacency inevitable. However, the changing economic climate is forcing even non-profit institutions to look to expansion and an external clientele.

The US for-profit universities and the now privately-owned GATE remain the major lobbyists for faster resolution of the WTO 1994 agreement on recognising education as a tradeable commodity. There are complex regulatory and international issues involved, which go to the heart of national interests, quality regimes, and funding mechanisms to support the public subsidy of education. Professional associations such as accountants and architects are already smoothing different national accreditation requirements, and it may be that their moves, shaping as they do higher education curricula, will do more to standardise higher education provision and global education than the ongoing negotiations over GATS. Nevertheless, there remains strong opposition to global education at the labour level, with Education International, a confederation of 300 teacher unions recently reasserting their rejection of the WTO stance. Whatever the truth of statements such as Urdan and Heggens observation that 'The world is hungry for education made in America', there are few indications of a stampede to the trough. At Pennsylvania State

University, where its World Campus was launched to great fanfare in 1998, only 3 per cent of the 3500 annual student enrolments are international, with the great majority from the eight most populous states surrounding Pennsylvania, and one-third enrolled in a non-credit WebMaster Certificate level programme, WC's most popular programme.

World Campus also benefited from a US$982 000 grant from the Learning Anywhere Anytime Partnerships (LAAP) programme to develop their courses, with in-kind support from Apple and Sun. Indeed, it cannot be stressed enough how much technological initiatives in US universities have benefited from relatively enormous grants by Australian standards, and from the generosity of philanthropic foundations. The Alfred P. Sloan Foundation alone has provided over US$35 million in grant support for online education ventures since 1992, most of them using an interactive not independent learning model. While some education consultants continue to 'talk up' the potential of global markets in education, and organisations such as the World Bank promote the use of 'exported' educational products while insisting on at least partial local ownership of the 'distribution channels', or local learning centres, other observers are more cautious. Stokes (2001), for example, tellingly places a question mark in his assessment of the potential of a globalised education sector, and his list of 13 major global 'players' includes only one company whose core business is degree education, Apollo, owner of UoP. The others are publishers, or training/service companies such as SmartForce.

The challenges associated with global expansion should not be underestimated, notes Stokes, and include the difficulties of intellectual property developed through joint ventures with local companies in states where the legal system is yet to offer protection, repatriation of profits in some regions, as well as adaptation of curriculum. Stokes' summary does not consider the cultural, pedagogical and philosophical issues associated with distance education in many cultures, we believe these remain pertinent. One company has recognised some of the 'soft issues' involved in borderless education: Sylvan's international strategy is to focus not on its content divisions, but on its service operations, since these are 'exportable'. Whether they too are culture free is a moot point. The pull of a global presence in higher education makes membership of consortia of institutions with similar interests an attractive possibility for some in higher education. Consortia have been made possible by internet-based communication, and made necessary by the high cost of multimedia and web-enhanced teaching and learning.

Although the majority of these consortia are still national, there is an increasing trend, often led by institutions outside the US but including several US institutions, to international collaboration. One national example is JesuitNET, a three-year project of 25 US Jesuit institutions, including the long-established distance education Regis College. The Association of Jesuit Colleges and Universities has partnered with IBM to develop a software programme, which can record how students solve problems online, how it might assess online competency-based education (a particular strength at Regis). AJCU will jointly develop online subjects incorporating the particular emphases of Jesuit educational philosophy.

Although immediate benefits are expected for the

subscribing members in terms of sharing resources and increasing student numbers across the consortium, a longer-term strategy is commercialisation of the software. Blackboard is the platform used. Eleven British and US research institutions, including the Universities of Bristol, Manchester and Illinois at Urbana-Champaign, have formed the Worldwide Universities Network to bid for a portion of the UK e-university, but there are also plans for a web-based graduate school by 2002. Partnerships for teaching are another emerging feature, for example, the University of Pennsylvania's Wharton Business School has announced a partnership with France's INSEAD campuses in Fontainebleau and Singapore to expand their global continuing and executive education. Franchising and licensing of programmes are other strategic moves employed in the quest for global expansion. For example, Scottish Knowledge, part-owned by News Corporation, markets Heriot-Watt University's web-enhanced ScholarTutor university preparation programme. The latter has been adopted by the Open University of Malaysia for its foundation Science course.

Some interesting data are emerging regarding the likelihood of long-term interest in global university degree programmes. As many governments begin to respond to internationalisation and globalisation agendas, and students themselves become more mobile, student flows have increased. Although postgraduate study at centres of international excellence has long been a feature of tertiary education, especially for those intent on an academic career, directed mobility programmes are now attracting undergraduate students in larger numbers. UK student numbers in US institutions have steadily increased to over 8000 in 2000, half undergraduate. Johnson reveals that Science and Engineering postgraduates (including IT students) in both the UK and US are increasingly seeing research study as an entrée into the labour force of the host country, with, for example, no Irish students returning to Ireland within 12 months after completion of the doctoral degree, and in the US, low return rates for Indian and Chinese graduates. This may suggest a strategic motivation on the part of students seeking better employment prospects to seek migration via further studies.

This would militate against take-up of online degree programmes, leaving the field to the short coursework programmes also targeted by the corporate and for-profit providers. Moreover, a number of commentators are noting more determined moves by many countries to develop their own distance learning initiatives. China Central Radio and Television University, for example, with 1.5 million students and a synchronous broadcast model, is now training staff at the Open University of Hong Kong, in an effort to introduce more flexible delivery modes. However, online provision remains a challenge in China as in most developing countries, where computer access is a major inhibiting factor in mass education efforts. Following the January 2001 founding of the Arab Open University, which has links to the UKOU, Jordan's public Hashemite University recently announced plans for a US$20 million Arab American University for Distance Learning, to begin in late 2002, specifically catering for the Middle Eastern population as well as Arab expatriates; it is to provide a Muslim perspective but to specialise in IT.

Although Hashemite currently has only 7000 students, the Jordanian authorities predict the external university will enrol 10 000 students in its first year. Half of the money would come from a private Kuwaiti firm. This announcement of a 'virtual university' sponsored by the state echoes the comments made above in relation to state belief in the potential of virtual universities, with assistance from private partnership funding. Apart from Thomson's links with U21, there is little evidence of much enthusiasm from private equity partners for global education ventures. More countries are also imposing stricter controls over foreign distance programmes. South Africa has strict regulations in place for higher education institutions, and India is also in the process of demanding registration of all providers. Brazil has refused to recognise any foreign-sponsored qualifications. In Malaysia, tax breaks previously available to parents sending children abroad for education have been withdrawn, forcing more students to remain in country, and more to consider the distance programmes set up by government.

There are other cautionary signals in the take-up of global distance education provision. The first is the questionable demand for for-credit higher education in developed economies in an increasingly fragmented Knowledge Economy. The growth of the for-profit market in higher education was predicated on a population demographic of advanced economies that suggested that the baby boomer group, excluded from prior higher education, was increasingly recognising the value of higher education for its upwardly mobile aspirations. There were also predictions of higher education participation rates among the bulge of 'echo boomers', attracted by the 'private good returns' of further education and the increased access available in a mass education system as a result of heavy investment in the university system in the 1970s.

However, recent figures from the UK indicate that the early rush of mature age students to part-time programmes has declined as a result of the introduction of tuition fees, and a buoyant labour market. Goddard analyses a Funding Council, Supply and Demand in Higher Education, indicating that growth in full-time undergraduate enrolment had declined since 1993 despite a population growth in the school leaver cohort, that part-time undergraduate and sub-degree level enrolments had not achieved their targets in 2000, and mature age numbers fell 1995-2000, although enrolments have risen slightly in the new academic year 2001. In the later age group, Engineering and Technology courses enrolments dropped, along with numbers in the physical sciences, with only small growth in IT and medical studies. Non-traditional populations were still not seeking further education, notwithstanding the advent of new institutions and alternate pathways to higher education, and the expanded places in new institutions. Rather, expansion was placing pressure on old 'brand name' institutions.

The same decline in enrolments was seen in 2000 figures in further education, with drops in both school leaver and adult cohorts, down by 1.8 per cent. This does not, however, gainsay the demand in the developing world. The second factor is the limited take-up of exclusively online degree study, even from 'brand' institutions, as employers question the credibility of solely online programs for developing soft skills. 37 per cent of Human Resources officials were reluctant to accept online graduate degrees, prompting Cathy Gunn, the Director of the Illinois Virtual Campus, a broker for 62 state colleges and universities, to decry the public perception that e-learning is 'easier', and to initiate a massive marketing campaign for distance education.

The failure of a supply-driven model, at least in generic online products such as the MBA. At a national US level, online and distance programmes constitute only 2.5 per cent of total MBA enrolments in 2000, with more than half of these in UoP's programme, reflecting both the attraction of its brand in the convenience rather than prestige market, and UoP's superior focus on online delivery.

There are several elements in the credibility problem suffered by distance award programmes. The first relates to the perception that online education, like distance education more generally, is a poor experience:

> People have taken to the net quicker than any previous household technology. Still, e-education lags far behind other online activities, such as gathering travel or health information. The promise of e-learning is great; the barriers, beginning with public trust are as many.

The founder of smarthinking, the troubled online tutorial company, observed in an interview that 'some people thought it would be easier to change people's behaviour than it really is. The technology is there, but the economics, the organisation, and the behaviours of people take far longer to change.... Technology is the easy part.' Even in non-award programmes, and notwithstanding early claims of massive savings to corporations, few e-learning vendors have been able to verify purported ROI on investment in learning programmes. Indeed Chen in his Eduventures, on Return on Investment, argues that only one case was able to demonstrate convincing ROI for e-learning programmes, and only four companies, IBM Mindspan, Digital Think, Docent and Saba, were able to assist corporations in even evaluating ROI. In corporate America, the effectiveness of e-learning was still largely determined by take-up across the organisation, and reduced travel/accommodation costs, not insignificant measures, but hardly reflective of efficacy.

The second relates to online technology itself. BBE noted that notwithstanding the hype and boosterism attached to online distance education, videoconferencing, television broadcast with audio-response capacity, and teleconferencing remain popular forms of delivery for 'distributed' learning, because the nature of such distance modes does not challenge the 'comfort zone' of either staff or students, since it replicates the oral/visual lecture/tutorial format. It has been argued that the numbers involved in such delivery modes are higher than those in web-based only programmes. Shive and Dirr found that live interactive video remained the most popular delivery mode at the end of the century. Certainly the University of Maine's distance enrolments reflect a telecourse enrolment of four times its online enrolment numbers, though the latter are growing sharply. Other institutions are making the difficult decision to abandon 'old technology' and migrate their video segments to the web, but the demand remains, and the technology is reliable and cheap for those institutions which invested in it in the 1970s. One large education provider, Learning Tree International, insists that no successful business model for e-learning has emerged, with the result that it would remain in classroom-based provision.

BBE noted that non-credit certificate programmes were already emerging as the most likely form of education for the business market, with the promise of the internet for 'anytime, anywhere, any place' study being more attractive for acquiring workplace-related skills through non-credit short courses in the training sector. This observation is supported by the recent work of Cliff Adelman, of the US Department of Education, in his research on certification programmes offered by software and hardware companies through franchise or internal training programmes. One recent indication that online certification programmes may enter Australia outside the established Novell, Microsoft and Sun distribution channels, is the recent announcement by eWebUniversity, an e-learning platform and content provider, that it would partner with San Jose State University to deliver IT certification courses into Australia. Details are as yet very sketchy, but Australia's shortage of IT specialists has led to perceptions of an under-served market. This trend to certification is a reflection of the move to knowledge management within organisations, and measurable outcomes from training, although a gap remains between ascertaining that employees have in fact learned something via assessment of their capabilities, and the ROI on training. However, there may be signs that the certification of IT skills is plateauing as well.

The Information Technology Association of America in April released a study. The number of job vacancies in IT dropped 44 percent from 1999, although this still left an estimated 425 000 jobs unfilled because of a lack of qualified staff. The best job preparation for skills and knowledge in software engineering, database development and technical writing, though graduates of private technical schools offering certificates were preferred by employers for network design and digital media production. More significantly, non-IT companies preferred employees with a degree qualification, while IT companies (those developing IT) ranked certifications at least as highly as a degree. The ITAA pointed out that there are 300 000 more non-IT than IT companies in the US, indicating that the employment preferences of the majority of employers should be a greater guide to work preparation for most students. In summary, as recession looms in most economies in late 2001, it remains to be seen whether fear of unemployment will translate into a growth in education and training enrolments. Most educators and analysts suggest a surge as unemployed adults retrain, but increased personal contributions to tuition in major economies, and higher tuition costs, may well deter individuals, and as argued above, corporations have resorted to layoffs rather than retraining, and are likely to delay the new product development which drives most company training.

Staffing issues

In 2000, we noted the growth in the number of part-time and casual teaching staff within US higher education institutions. This trend has increased, with part-timers constituting 45 per cent of staff 1998-99, compared to 40 per cent in 1992-93 and salary gaps widening between private and public institutions, and between tenured and non-tenured staff. One US study found that 34 per cent of all undergraduate subjects were taught by graduate students. In reaction, Teaching Assistants, who are in most cases graduate students with high teaching loads, have begun to unionise at many campuses, for higher pay and lower contact hours, with some success. There is also a large increase in the number of institutions not offering tenured positions, from 8 per cent of institutions to 14 percent over the same period, reflecting the funding pressures on non-profit universities to alter employment conditions. In Australia, the casualisation of the workforce has also increased since the BBE, with nearly 90 percent of teaching-only staff designated as casual, and 18 per cent of all academic staff. Hence the contrast between 'traditional universities' and for-profit institutions in the 2000, has become less stark in relation to the use of part-time and casual teaching staff.

Meanwhile, in corporate universities, staff salaries account for a mere 31 per cent of operating costs, a significant difference from labour costs in more traditional institutions, and an indication that the proportion of institutional costs spent on staffing has some way to go before it reaches this industry level. The debate on the role of the teacher in higher education has intensified as online methods of delivery have become more embedded into standard programmes. As e-learning providers themselves concede the ineffectiveness of many of their earlier stand-alone and generic online courses, it is more widely recognised that quality internet-based learning requires more than 'information delivery', and depends on the interactive dimension provided by a participating teacher, who provides the dialogue that Laurillard has argued is essential for education.

Student Issues

'Convenience', 'student-centred service' and condensed programming are three significant lessons traditional universities have quickly learned from the new providers, as university administrators perceive that higher education is 'a consumer led market'. US research indicating an increased instrumentalist attitude to education, which might suggest even stronger growth in 'no frills' degree provision. Almost two years' worth of experience in student reactions to electronic teaching modes, distributed and online learning, and changes in on-campus attendance patterns. Three significant trends can be discerned.

The first is growing evidence of high attrition, at 60-80 per cent, in asynchronous non-award online generic programmes in IT and business, even where these are supported by employers, to the extent that the Masie Center and the American Society for Training and Development surveyed students and employers, and considered financial incentives might be necessary. Frankola, of NYUOnline, agrees; in her experience, some face-to-face sessions in the course are also vital for completion because of the value students perceive in proximal learning communities. This desire for social interaction may be particularly acute in work-related learning, as suggested by several commentators in the 2000.

Others argue that assessment of company training would increase completion. Both elements of course leach the cost savings that e-learning promised the corporate sector, and eliminate the own-time convenience of asynchronous learning. There is also a growing concern that virtual work-related learning is no panacea for either employer or employee simply because it is 'anytime, anywhere', and thus intrudes into already crowded work and domestic routines. However, were assessment attached to company training, it would increase the pressure on education providers to credit their company training into award programmes.

Second, attrition rates in for-credit programmes appear to be more promising: State's World Campus courses have a 95 per cent completion rate, while UCLA have improved their retention rate to 85-89 percent because of the high level of interactivity supported by the University, via both course managers and instructors, and the insistence of the University that instructors undergo five to six weeks of intensive training in preparation for online teaching, as well as a mandated online time of five days a week several times a day to respond to questions and guide discussion. At the associate degree level, the figures are not so encouraging: in California, the community college sector distance completion rates 13 per cent below those for on-campus programmes. Third, there is some evidence of the emergence of resistance in on-campus undergraduate courses to decreasing contact time, larger classes and lack of 'real' laboratory classes, the transactional aspects of education conceived as more than information delivery. Students, it appears, want the choice of flexible attendance, but are unhappy when face-to-face sessions are reduced.

Of critical interest to university funding agencies and managers in Australia is the issue of student response to online forms of learning, and student expectations of on-campus study. Flexible delivery of programmes, made possible by the new technologies, have combined with changing social attitudes and patterns of connection among school leavers to alter the nature of higher education. It is therefore difficult to extricate the extent to which online education provision, sometimes confused with flexible delivery, is a response to actual demand by students, or a supply-push mechanism by commercial vendors and university managers seeking supplementary income and reduced costs. Most likely, it is both, although as indicated, students in the main are concerned at the prospect of diminished choice in relation to on-campus classes.

Disengagement' from the campus experience consequent on increased paid work commitments, increasing access to digital resources, and flexible programming. McInnes warns against a simple response to 'student demand', which might abrogate university responsibility to determine optimal curriculum design and learning experiences at the undergraduate level. Yet universities must also resist the temptations to ignore the reality of student lives, and to persist with a 'romantic' vision of the ideal student experience. One might posit a shift in university attendance and engagement, which more closely mirrors that of the old apprenticeship model of blended work/study, particularly as universities themselves seek to incorporate more workplace-based training in their professional programmes. This may have the effect of establishing lifelong learning, conceived as a constant renewal of work work work work work skills, as a standard education 'system'

More immediately, it is also likely to extend the period of enrolment for undergraduate and postgraduate students, and increase administrative costs by spreading students over a longer time to graduation, unless units are reconceptualized via curriculum design to the short course, six-week UoP model. For McInnes, one implication of a lack of student engagement is the necessity to re-assert the value of a coherent and cohesive curriculum.

Intellectual property issues

The confusing and complex state of IP in US universities is well-exemplified in an interview with Kenneth Salomon in University Business. Salomon argues that academia is currently protected by exception from the work-for-hire rule that assigns copyright to the employer if the employee is tenured, or the digitisation of his/her knowledge is performed as part of expected work duties. However, the situation is vastly complicated by the input of other institutional employees into the digitisation process, as, for example, graphics illustrators, as well aBs the matter of students copying notes and then posting them for sale on the web. For educational institutions, the critical issue is to agree and implement a policy on ownership and/or use of materials, including the right to amend any future use of the materials, and right to use after the originator leaves the institution. Some universities such as the University of North Texas now have agreements allocating royalties to staff producing online materials, although the amount depends on how much assistance was provided by the university. We documented the Arthur Miller case at Harvard, where Arthur Miller produced teaching materials for another Law School, and Harvard objected. Salomon argues that this 'wasn't a copyright issue per se; it was a conflict of interest and conflict of commitment to Harvard', that should have been addressed in terms of employee exclusivity arrangements.

At the institutional level, a major breakthrough in digital copyright law has been achieved with the TEACH (Technology, Education and Copyright Harmonisation) Act. This allows only non-profit educational providers to digitise materials that would normally be used to support face-to-face classes for limited-time online access by bona fide students. For-profit providers will continue to pay for copyright, which is a further reason many are anxious to partner with e-publishers. The onus then is on individual universities to negotiate with employees regarding the 'ownership' of teaching materials. However, the broader issues associated with IP in borderless education remain a matter for caution.

Curriculum Issues

A number of commentators in the 2000, flagged the issue of curriculum control as critical to the future of public higher education as corporate, virtual and for-profit entities expanded, and as non-profit educational institutions struggled with falling public funding. Watkins (Council of Higher Education Associations, CHEA) and Mingle (SHEEO) noted that thus far, the community college sector was most susceptible to corporate influence on curriculum and pedagogical practice, since the mission at VET level is to be industry-responsive, but also because corporations could exercise direct financial pressure. However, there is now growing evidence of curriculum change within universities, both in response to student demand for incorporation of job-relevant certifications and of vendor deals, which provide equipment in return for use of their certification programmes. Hence proprietary, corporate or for-profit institutional online training programmes are incorporated into accredited degree programmes, as the California State University has agreed to do for a networking training programme developed by Alcatel, in return for lab equipment and teaching staff from Alcatel. Other institutions, such as Colorado State and Georgia State, are incorporating such proprietary products as SkillSoft's web-based self-paced offerings, in their continuing education courses. The same trend is already present in Australia, in such programmes as Cisco certification as a component of the QUT IT degree. The President of one community college which welcomes NETg's free courseware distributed through Michigan Virtual University, recognises the issues this raises in terms of the integrity of curriculum, and accreditation:

> Colleges and universities must learn to adjust and make decisions about how to incorporate programmes like this into their credentialing processes. This is not an isolated incident. It's the dawn of a new age in high-quality, web-based curriculum that's commercially prepared.

Such deals raise the issue of quality and coherence of the curriculum, as well as who teaches these components, and flags the entry of more complex curriculum decision-making at departmental level, as staff consider whether what amounts to training leaches the cognitive capacities of students because of the performative performative performative performative performative emphasis of certification.

Administrators of online programs assume consumers want a bite-sized 'point and click' accumulation of facts rather than a more reflective, less easily measured search for knowledge. It's also wrong to assume that all student customers know entirely what they need in an education program and what kind of material will lead to the desired educational product.

Credit transfer, is a further challenge to curriculum integrity. UoP, that their incoming students have accrued as many as five unit equivalents from different institutions, and equivalence is determined at institutional, not faculty level. This would suggest that the previous reliance on individual academic expertise to ensure the quality of degree composition has been further eroded, and that we must seriously question the notion of what a degree in a particular discipline might mean. To date, little attention has been given to curriculum matters: O'Donoghue and Twigg are two of the few who note it as critical in the development of private/ public partnerships and consortia of providers. Certainly we can discern a major shift away from the traditional 'input measures' of quality such as qualifications of the faculty teaching subjects, and the number of books in the library. Further, the increase in global university consortia, agreeing on common core curricula, places further pressure on the academic preference for distinct and self-generated curricula within individual institutions. As memoranda on joint curricula are agreed at the institutional level, the 'not-invented-here syndrome' becomes increasingly harder to maintain at the individual academic level.

When curricula are shared between institutions, supported by major publishers, and the design and development component of academic work becomes more centralised (as in the for-profit institutions), greater attention will focus on the role of teaching as a central role for academics, and the issue of training for, and the accreditation of, teaching will gain greater prominence in the higher education context.

Technology Developments

Many of the technical problems associated with online

learning remain, notwithstanding predictions that interoperability of various platforms would be achieved quickly, and bandwidth would increase dramatically in response to demand. Where in 1999 and 2000, debate swirled about the efficacy of 'distributed' or distance education via new technologies, and whether or not cost efficiencies could be achieved, there is now growing recognition that quality education on the web will not significantly reduce costs, that hybrid modes are required for retention of students, and effective learning, and that early predictions of productivity gains, improved quality of learning outcomes, and cost reductions have proved difficult to demonstrate with any validity, when each is added to the ROI equation.

However, Urdan and Weggen, 14 per cent decline in interactive web-based training in 1999 over the previous year, indicating that as margins tightened in the e-learning market, vendors were reverting to static, generic and asynchronous uses of the web and the internet. The very aspects of online learning that promised to revolutionise learning, and that most experts recognise as fundamental to motivation and retention, such as live interactivity from a distance, customisation, streaming media and so on, have become prohibitive in terms of cost. The critical issue is that interactivity is thus far not scaleable. While the notion of '24/7' service has become standard rhetoric, the reality in most online programmes is somewhat different: certainly access to digital resources is common on a continuous basis at most institutions, but few have managed the resourcing necessary to enable day-long tutorial or technical assistance.

As indicated above, the major technological challenge for most institutions is integrating the various software programmes for different functional areas of their operations. It has certainly occupied far more administrative time and far more of the operational budget than tentative moves into online teaching, although media attention has focused on the more dramatic change signalled by e-learning. The Connecticut State University system, for example, is still struggling with implementation of a software programme that has consumed five years in development and implementation, and is several million dollars over budget. The costs of implementing administrative software remain huge: the University of British Columbia has spent C$12 million over five years to introduce PeopleSoft. Canadian universities entering the overseas market 'tectonic clashes' between electronic administrative systems designed for local markets being unable to incorporate international funds transfers, and student complaints regarding administrative systems outnumbering academic complaints by 10:1.

Furthermore, the range of services demanded by a 'client centred focus' in universities has changed, as students demand faster access to resources, the ability to transfer funds electronically, and the ability to access tuition aid programmes online. Administrative systems must be adapted to accommodate online teaching and learning, and this is proving difficult. Consequently, costs have increased because universities must maintain dual paper/digital systems. There are other difficulties of a cultural nature: Gartner Group Vice President Michael Zastrocky, that only 2 per cent of US non-profit education providers use an external host system for information systems because of continuing concern about security issues.

Although a number of analysts, for example Hambrecht and Co, predict the demise of the CDROM and video as delivery mechanisms, publishers do not seem to agree: core textbooks increasingly come as hybrid products of text and accompanying CDROM. Nor is there any indication of students spurning print text: indeed Prof. Shirley Alexander's current research at the University of Technology, Sydney, indicates a strong resistance to screen reading, and a strong desire to print any screen information. E-books, through deals with web publishing software makers such as Adobe Systems. Adobe's eBook University initiative of mid-2001 involves a partnership with nine institutions, including MIT's Sloan School of Management, the University of Maryland University College, and the University of Wisconsin (the latter two amongst the largest distance education providers in the US), to provide texts through Adobe's eBook Reader. Students will be able to download the Reader for free from publishers' websites, or a bookstore with an online purchase of the text. Adobe has secured agreement from all major publishers for the initiative, which promises cost savings on warehousing of physical texts and distribution costs. However, student acceptance of e-texts is not a foregone conclusion. At the same time, digital publishers are looking to for-profit providers to encourage e-books. Apollo has signed an exclusive agreement to use Microsoft Reader, and to ultimately offer all texts digitally.

Analysts suggest that the adoption of a proprietary reader platform is crucial to penetration. However, publisher-exclusive deals with one reader platform would seem business suicide. Over the last two years, new technological developments have focused on the programming of learning objects, and digital publishing. Both are in the early stages of standardisation and commercial application. A critical issue in the digitising of learning resources remains the cost factor, and 'legacy issues'. As museums and universities seek to make their rich resources available to a wider public, the costs of the process, and the maintenance of dual physical and virtual collections, along with the fact that there is no current solution to changing technical platforms and the preservation of current digitised resources, are proving major challenges.

One ironic footnote on technological developments might suggest some caution on the part of universities introducing wireless internet access on-campus. Two private US colleges, Bentley and Babson, have been obliged to block internet access to their lecture theatres during classes, because students were surfing and emailing rather than 'paying attention'. A further caution is the increasing tendency of US students to download huge video and music files, jamming servers, increasing university costs, and potentially opening the university to copyright breaches. Student demand has forced many universities such as the University of Denver to double bandwidth, install 'shapers' to limit entertainment downloads via peer-to-peer file-sharing.

Quality Assurance Issues

A major issue in the area of policy remains the issue of quality control of degree study as the internet makes cross-border provision of education relatively easy for dodgy providers. This is not an issue confined to Australia, but it is one that has thus far found no simple solution; Twigg describes online quality processes as 'chaos' from a student perspective. Contreras provides a brief update on the activities of some of the exposed diploma mills; for example, Columbia Pacific University was closed down in California, was re-established in Montana as Columbia Commonwealth University, and has also been 'accredited' in Malawi. Montana does not legislate private provision of higher education. Variations in state regulations allow questionable operators to locate in states such as Wyoming and Hawaii, which are lax in their regulatory environments. One institution, Preston University has a majority of its students in Pakistan, but is based in Wyoming.

Another previously fraudulent operator, La Salle University in Louisiana, was bought out and 'legitimised' in 1997 after nearly 10 years' operation. It established a sister provider, Orion College, which however, has attracted fewer than 100 students by end-2000, prompting its chief academic officer to note ruefully: 'When you go legitimate, the sad thing is that it is not a good thing for the money situation'. Not even the imprimatur of an accrediting agency in the US is guaranteed to provide consumer protection: The Chronicle of Higher Education lists three spurious accrediting committees, including the American Council of Private Colleges and Universities. It is evident that neither legal nor systemic regulatory systems have been able to keep pace with the rapid advances made in technology over the last decade. The Napster case is a prime example. The e-learning and for-profit education environment has demonstrated that current quality assurance systems are inadequate to deal not merely with unscrupulous providers, but more significantly, that they are not addressing the many different issues involved in distributed learning.

This has prompted organisations such as the Commonwealth of Learning and the Pew Learning and Technology Program to convene symposia to tackle the many issues involved in quality assurance. At the same time, the number of 'best practice guidelines' for online education provision has proliferated. Labour organisations such as the National Education Association and the American Federation of Teachers ('Distance Education Guidelines for Good Practice', have outlined their approaches, along with regional accrediting bodies (such as the Council of Regional Accrediting Committees), and WICHE. The Institute of Higher Education Policy has also published a commissioned study, 'Quality on the line: Benchmarks for success in internet-based distance eduction'. Ryan summarises some of these. What is clear is that traditional quality assurance systemic measures are no longer adequate for the new educational environment, with its blurred borders between informal and formal learning, online and on-campus provision, and a greater emphasis on outcomes-based assessment.

2

Trade Barriers

The GATS is the first ever set of multilateral rules covering international trade in services. Previous international trade agreements covered trade in products, but never services.

The GATS was negotiated in the Uruguay Round and came into effect in 1995. It is administered by the World Trade Organization (WTO) which is made up of 144 member countries.

The World Trade Organization (WTO) is the only global international organization dealing with the rules of trade between nations. At its heart are the WTO agreements, negotiated and signed by the majority of the world's trading nations and ratified in their parliaments.

The GATS is one of these key agreements and is a legally enforceable set of rules. The GATS has three parts. The first part is the framework that contains the general principles and rules. The second part consists of the national schedules that list a country's specific commitments on access to their domestic market by foreign providers. The third part consists of annexes which detail specific limitations for each sector can be attached to the schedule of commitments. This will be discussed in more detail later, but first it is essential to understand what kind of education services will be covered by GATS and what is meant by higher education services.

Modes of Trade in Services

The GATS defines four ways in which a service can be traded, known as 'modes of supply'. These four modes of trade apply to all service sectors in GATS.

Categories of education services

Trade in education is organized into five categories or sub-sectors of service. These categories are based on the United Nations Provisional Central Product Classification (CPC). The three categories that are most relevant to this report are 'higher', 'adult' and 'other'. The four modes of service described above apply to each of the categories. Critics of this classification system believe that it does not reflect the reality of today where non-traditional and private providers exist and alternate forms of delivery using new technologies are being used. However, countries are able to add their own qualifications or supplements to the UN CPC classification scheme and therefore, in principle, should not be limited by the scheme.

Key elements and rules of the GATS

The overall framework contains a number of general obligations applicable to all trade in services regardless of whether a country has made a specific commitment to sectors or not. These are called unconditional obligations. Fundamental to this discussion is the Most Favoured Nation (MFN) rule. Each WTO member lists in its national schedules those services for which it wishes to provide access to foreign providers. In addition to choosing which service sector/s will be committed, each country determines the extent of commitment by specifying the level of market access and the degree of national treatment they are prepared to guarantee.

Controversial Questions and issues related to higher education

The GATS is described as a voluntary agreement because countries can decide which sectors they will agree to cover under GATS rules. This is done through the preparation of their national schedules of commitments and through the 'request-offer' negotiation rounds. However, there are aspects of the agreement that question its voluntary nature, notably the built-in progressive liberalization agenda and other elements described in this section. Probably, the most controversial and critical issue related to the agreement is the meaning of Article 1.3. This article defines which services are covered or exempted. According to the WTO, the agreement is deemed to apply to all measures affecting services except "those services supplied in the exercise of governmental authority". But what does 'exercise of governmental authority' mean? GATS supporters maintain that education provided and funded by the government is therefore exempted. Sceptics question the broad interpretation of the clause and ask for more a detailed analysis.

The agreement states that "in the exercise of governmental authority" means the service is provided on a 'non-commercial basis' and 'not in competition' with other service suppliers. This begs the follow-up question - what is meant by non-commercial basis and not in competition? These issues are at the heart of much of the debate about which services are covered. Education critics of the GATS maintain that due to the wide-open interpretation of 'non-commercial' and 'not in competition' terms, the public sector/government service providers may not in fact be exempt.

The situation is especially complicated in those countries where there is a mixed public/private higher education system or where a significant amount of funding for public institutions in fact comes from the private sector. Another complicationis that a public education institution in an exporting country is often defined as private/commercial when it crosses the border and delivers in the importing country.

Therefore, one needs to question what 'non-commercial' really means in terms of higher education trade. The debate about what 'not in competition' means is fuelled by the fact that there does not appear to be any qualifications or limits on the term. For instance, if non-government providers (private non-profit or commercial) are delivering services, are they deemed to be in competition with government providers?

In this scenario, public providers may be defined as being 'in competition' by the mere existence of non-governmental providers. Does the method of delivery influence or limit the concept of 'in competition'? Does the term cover situations where there is a similar mode of delivery, or for instance, does this term mean that public providersusing traditional face-to-face classroom methods could be seen to be competing with foreign for-profit e-learning providers? There are many unanswered questions that need clarification.

Supporters of the GATS emphasize that education is to a large extent a government function and that the agreement does not seek to displace the public education systems and the right of government to regulate and meet domestic policy objectives. Others express concern that the whole question of the protection of public services is very uncertain and potentially at risk in view of the narrow interpretation of what governmental authority means and a wide-open interpretation of what 'not in competition' and non- commercial basis' mean.

Clearly, the question -which higher and adult education 'services exercised in governmental authority' are exempted from GATS - needs to be front and centre in the debate on the risks and opportunities associated with the agreement.· What does the principle of progressive liberalization mean? GATS is not a neutral agreement. It aims to promote and enforce the liberalization of trade in services. The process of progressive liberalization involves two aspects- extending GATS coverage to more service sectors and decreasing the number and extent of measures that serve as impediments to increased trade.

Therefore, in spite of the right of each country to determine the extent of its commitments, with each new round of negotiations, countries are expected to add sectors or sub-sectors to their national schedules of commitments and to negotiate the further removal of limitations on market access and national treatment.

The intention of GATS is to facilitate and promote evermore opportunities for trade. Therefore, countries that are not interested in either the import or export of education services will most likely experience greater pressures to allow market access to foreign providers. GATS is a very new instrument and it is too soon to predict thereality or extent of these potential opportunities or risks.

At the 'request-offer' stage of the process, there are bilateral negotiations on market access and national treatment commitments. The key point at this step, is that sectors for which access is sought do not have to correspond to those for which requests are made. So country A may request of Country B greater access to transportation services. Country B can respond by requesting access to education services. It is up to each country as to where they are willing to make concessions on foreign access to domestic markets. This situation applies to all sectors and may be of greatest concern to countries, developing or developed, who have not made commitments to open up education services and might therefore consider their education service sector vulnerable to negotiating deals across sectors. These issues relate to the mechanics and legalities of the agreement itself. Each one raises questions that need further clarification and analysis and collectively they serve to wave the red flag that more attention needs to be given to these matters. There are other aspects of the GATS, such as the dispute mechanism, subsidies, treatment of monopolies which are controversial and apply to all sectors and which need further study.

Article 6.4, which addresses measures relating to qualification requirements and procedures, technical standards and licensing requirements may have serious implications for education and requires further clarification. It must be remembered that GATS is still anuntested agreement and a certain amount of confusion exists on how to interpret the major rules and obligations. It took many years to iron out the inconsistencies in the General Agreement on Tariffs and Trade (GATT) and the same will likely be true for GATS. While trade specialists and lawyers need to review the technical and legal aspects of the agreement, it is educators who need to study how the agreement applies to and impacts education services.

Commitments to Trade in Education Services

Extent of country commitments

The education sector is one of the least committed sectors. The reason is not clear, but perhaps it can be attributed to the need for countries to strike a balance between pursuing domestic education priorities and exploring ways in which trade in education services can be further liberalized. Or it could be linked to the fact that to date, education, in general, has taken a very low priority in the major bilateral agreements and rightly or wrongly, the same may be true for the GATS.

Only 44 of the 144 WTO Members have made commitments to education, and only 21 of these have included commitments to higher education. It is interesting to note that Congo, Lesotho, Jamaica and Sierra Leone have made full unconditional commitments in higher education, perhaps with the intent of encouraging foreign providers to help develop their educational systems.

Australia's commitment for higher education covers provision of private tertiary education services, including university level. The European Union has included higher education in their schedule with clear limitations on all modes of trade except 'consumption abroad', which generally means foreign tuition paying students. Only three (USA, New Zealand, Australia) of the 21 countries with higher education commitments have submitted a negotiating proposal outlining their interests and issues. The next section provides a brief summary of key elements of the three proposals.

Analysis of negotiating proposals

Role of government

It is clear that all three proposals acknowledge the central role government plays in higher education. Perhaps the controversy about which public services are exempted from the GATS has prompted this explicit recognition of the government role. Some are comforted and appeased by these statements. Others are even more concerned about the potential erosion of the role of government in higher education provision and the setting of domestic policy objectives. In some countries, education is decentralized from national to provincial or state governmental bodies. Private education, though nominally under state authority, may not be primarily governed or regulated by a government. These situations further illustrate the complexities involved in determining which services are exempted from GATS coverage and the very different impact GATS will have on individual countries.

Rationales and benefits

The rationales that drive further liberalization differ from country to country. Australia stresses greater access for students, New Zealand points to economic and social benefits and the USA focuses on opportunities for new knowledge and skills. Benefits are closely linked to rationales. Australia believes that the competition inherent in more trade will have flow-on benefits to students. New Zealand emphasizes that in addition to revenue generation there are benefits at the individual, institutional and societal level through academic exchange,technological transfer and cross-cultural linkages.

The USA highlights the contribution to global spread of the modern knowledge economy and improved competitiveness. It is not a surprise that the economic benefits are emphasized but it is noteworthy that social and academic value to individuals, institutions and society are not totally overlooked. More work is needed to understand and analyse the perceived rationale and benefits as this will lead to a clearer picture of what countries expect from increased import and export in education. Of course, expectations can be seen in terms of desirable or undesirable results. A better understanding of anticipated outcomes would assist in the development of policies to help achieve or prevent them. At the same time, it is equally important to be mindful of 'unintended consequences'.

Public/private mix

The public/private mix of higher and adult education provision is implicitly and explicitly recognized in the proposals. It is interesting to note that New Zealand suggests that education may be one of the least committed service sectors due to the recognition of its 'public good' element and the high degree of government involvement in its provision. The USA is more pointed when they state that private education co-exists with the public domain and will continue to supplement, not displace public education systems. There are mixed reactions to this statement and a great deal of uncertainty as to how the GATS will affect the balance of a mixed system, especially given the individualized nature of mixed systems.

Further analysis needed

Further analysis of the factors driving commitments or the lack of commitments in higher education is needed. There are diverse perspectives on the number and substance of commitments because countries have different national policy objectives and therefore different goals and expectations from trade in education services. For example, a consumer oriented rationale can be interpreted as the need to provide a wider range of opportunities to consumers, or the need to protect consumers by assuring appropriate levels of access and quality. The economic rationale can be understood as a way to increase trade revenues for exporting countries or seen as a means to attract additional investment for education for importing countries. Other see the economic rationale as sabotaging the social development goals of education, or even scientific enquiry and scholarship. Any number of issues can be used to illustrate the debate and the dichotomy of opinions on the rationales and benefits of increased trade in education. Differences exist between and within countries and certainly among education groups as well. Further debate and analysis is necessary so that an informed position is taken on why or why not trade liberalization is attractive to an individual country and how trade agreements help or hinder achieving national goals and global interests.

Developing country interests

The voices of developing countries need to be heard so that the benefits and risks associated with increased trade are clear and do not undermine national efforts to develop and enhance domestic higher education. However, the voices and interests of the developing countries differ. The opportunity to have foreign suppliers provide increased access to higher and adult education programs or to invest in the infrastructure for education provision is attractive to some. The threat of foreign dominance or exploitation of a national system and culture is expressed by others. Trade liberalization for whose benefit or at what cost are key questions. Quality and accreditation are at the heart of much debate.

The importance of frameworks for licensing, accreditation, qualification recognition and quality assurance are important for all countries, whether they are importing and exporting education services. Developing countries have expressed concern about their capacity to have such frameworks in place in light of the push toward trade liberalization and increased cross border delivery of education. The GATS is one of many factors and instruments encouraging greater mobility of professionals. Although the agreement focuses on temporary movement of the labour force, it may lead to and facilitate permanent migration as well.

The implications of increased mobility of teachers and researchers are particularly relevant to developing countries. It will be a major challenge to improve education systems if well-qualified professionals and graduates are attracted to positions in other countries. At the root of the impact of GATS on developing countries is the fundamental issue of capacity to participate effectively in the global trading system and to be equal members in the WTO. Strong feelings exist about the potential for trade rules to make poor countries poorer, instead of narrowing the gap between developed and developing countries. The perceived injustice that poor nations are expected to remove trade barriers while rich nations retain barriers on certain goods, contributes to the strong reactions of some developing countries about the impact of GATS in general.

Barriers

Identification of the barriers to trade in higher education services is fundamental because it is the elimination of these barriers which is the raison d être of GATS. There are some barriers that are applicable to all sectors. There are other impediments that are specific to the education services sector. The following two sections list some of the generic barriers and also those most relevant to the four modes of trade in education. The sources used to identify these barriers are the three negotiating proposals described above, reports by non-governmental organizations (NGOs) and intergovernmental bodies, and by the WTO itself. This is a comprehensive collection of perceived barriers, not a list of the most significant ones. There is no agreement or consensus on which barriers are the most critical as they are usually seen from a self-interest perspective.

The list is for illustrative purposes only. Attention needs to be given to whether the barriers are seen from the perspective an exporting or importing country. Finally, it is important to remember that what is perceived as a barrier by some countries is perceived as fundamental to the education system in another.

The majority of these generic barriers are from an exporter country's point of view and focus on supply modes one and three.

- — lack of transparency of government regulatory, policy and funding frameworks·
- — domestic laws and regulations are administered in an unfair manner
- — subsidies are not made known in a clear and transparent manner
- — when government approval is required long delays are encountered and when approval is denied, no reasons are given for the denial and no information is given on what must be done to obtain approval in the future
- — tax treatment that discriminates against foreign suppliers
- — foreign partners are treated less favourably than other organizations.

Of course, many of these barriers are not new or specific to the GATS, as they already impact the flow of education services across borders. However, the barriers are significant as they are seen by some as key elements of a public education system that need to be maintained, and by others as impediments to trade. Some of the barriers identified above affect internationalization initiatives, in other words, those activities that do not have an economic or for-profit motive.

For instance, mobility of students and teachers for academic exchange or research purposes are affected by many of the barriers noted for supply modes two and four. It is important to note that within a country's schedule of commitments, it is possible to list specific limitations to market access and national treatment. These are a type of barrier and must be honoured. For example, Mexico has telecom laws that restrict the use of national satellites and receiving dishes. This has potential impact on cross border delivery of education services.

It is hard to predict what future barriers, especially technological ones, could be applied in order to control the electronic movement of education services across borders.

For instance, the capacity to install electronic fences may have major repercussions on cross border e-education. Finally, it should be mentioned that countries that have not made any formal commitments to trade in higher education services are currently in the process of easing some of the identified barriers.

A good example of this is the number of countries who are changing visa and employment requirements to attract more international students to study in their country. This is happening irrespective of the GATS.

Policy Issues and Questions

Given the current interest and pressure toward increasing trade liberalization, what are the policy implications that the higher education sector needs to look at? It is a challenging task to examine policy implications as the impact of trade liberalization is firmly enmeshed with other issues and trends in higher education. These trends include:

— the increasing use of ICTs for domestic and cross border delivery of programs

— the growing number of private for-profit entities providing higher education domestically and internationally

— the increasing tuition fees and other costs faced by students of public (and private) institutions,

— the need for public providers to seek alternate sources of funding which sometimes means engaging in for-profit activities or seeking private sector sources of financial support.

— the ability of government to fund the increasing demand for higher and adult education.

These trends are with us today in both developed and to some extent, developing countries. How does the existence of the GATS relate to these trends? While the GATS may lead to expanded use of electronic or distance education and may contribute to more commercial or market oriented approaches to education, it cannot be held responsible for the emergence or existence of these trends. Supporters of more trade in education services can celebrate the existence of the GATS to maximize the benefits of these trends and opportunities. Critics, on the other hand, can emphasize the risks associated with increased trade, believing that it leads to more for-profit providers, to programs of questionable quality, and to a market oriented approach - all of which are seen to challenge the traditional 'public good' approach to higher education. However, the impact of trade liberalizationon education cannot be positioned as an 'either-or' question or answer; it is a multi-layered and complex set of issues.

Role of government

The changing role of government is a contentious issues. First, let it be said that in general, globalization and the new public management are challenging and changing roles of government and nation state. The movement toward more trade liberalization is yet another factor. With respect to education, the government usually plays a role in the funding, regulation, monitoring and delivery of higher education or at least, designating bodies to do so. This is true in countries where a public system dominates or where a mixed public/private system exists. The advent of increased cross border delivery by foreign education providers raises the following issues all of which impact on the role of government:

— licensing and regulation procedures for foreign providers

— quality assurance and accreditation for imported and exported education services

— funding protocols including operating grants, loans, subsidies and scholarships

— qualification recognition and credit transfer systems

These issues will be discussed in more detail in other sections but the role of government as an education provider needs to be examined. A combination of increased demand for public services and limited financial capacity is forcing governments to examine their priorities and options for service delivery. In higher education, this has prompted a number of new developments. These include:

— developing funding formulas which are placing more of the financial burden on students

— forcing publicly funded institutions to seek alternate and additional sources of funds through entrepreneurial or commercial activities at home and abroad

— individual institutions wanting increased autonomy from government regulation

— permitting new private providers (non-profit and for-profit) to deliver specific education and training programs

These developments are further complicated if and when

a) a foreign public or private education provider is interested in access to the domestic market; and

b) if a domestic public provider is interested in seeking markets in other countries.

Together these scenarios require the government to take a long term and macro perspective on the impact of increased foreign trade on their role in the provision of and regulation of higher education.

Student Access

Many governments and public education institutions have keenly felt the responsibility of ensuring broad access to higher education opportunities. In many, if not in most countries, this is a challenging issue as the demand for higher and adult education is steadily growing, often beyond the capacity of the country to provide it. This is one more reason why some students are interested in out-of-country education opportunities and providers are prepared to offer higher education services across borders. When increased trade liberalization is factored into this scenario, the question of access becomes complicated. Advocates of liberalized trade maintain that consumers/students can have greater access to a wider range of education opportunities at home and abroad. Non-supporters of trade believe that access may in fact be more limited as trade will commercialize education, escalate costs and perhaps lead to a two-tiered system. Trade is therefore often perceived by critics as a threat to the 'public good' nature of education services. This raises the question of the capacity and role of government with respect to providing access to higher education.

For instance, if education is seen as a public function, can private providers or foreign providers help to fulfil this public function? If so, would foreign for-profit providers be eligible for the same grants, subsidies and tax incentives as public providers under the national treatment obligation of the GATS? Would this in turn decrease the amount of financial support available to public universities if funds were distributed across a larger number of institutions? Different education models exist and must exist in order to respond to the needs, resources and priorities of individual countries.

Funding

Many of the same issues and arguments regarding access can also apply to funding. Some governments have limited budget capacity or at least lack the political will to allocate funds to meet the needs of higher education. Can international trade provide alternate funding sources or new providers? Or, because of the GATS obligations such as most favoured nation treatment and national treatment obligations, does it mean that public funding will be spread too thinly across a broader set of domestic and foreign providers? Furthermore, does the presence of foreign providers signal to government that they can decrease public funding for higher and adult education, thereby jeopardizing domestic publicly funded institutions. Does international trade in education advantage some countries, such as those with well-developed capacity for export, and disadvantage others in terms of funding or access? Once again, the impact of more liberalized trade can be a double-edged sword with respect to funding, whether public or private, higher education teaching/learning and research activities.

Regulation of foreign or cross border providers

As already noted, a regulatory framework is needed to deal with the diversity of providers and new cross border delivery modes, and becomes more urgent as international trade increases. In some countries, this may mean a broader approach to policy which involves licensing, regulating and monitoring both private (profit and non-profit) and foreign providers to ensure that national policy objectives are met and public interests protected. It may also involve a shift in government and public thinking- while higher education remains a "public good", both public and private providers can fulfil this public function. This in turn may introduce greater competition among providers and general confusion for the consumer. Hence a coherent and comprehensive regulatory framework is called for- to serve national interests and protect the interests of different stakeholders, especially students. More work is necessary to determine how national regulatory frameworks are compatible with, or part of, a larger international framework. Increased connectivity and interdependence among nations, as well as liberalized trade, will mean urge greater coherence between national frameworks. How can coherence between a national framework and an international framework actually strengthen national regulatory and policy functions, not weaken them? Clearly there are risks and opportunities associated with this issue but doing nothing is a risk in itself.

Recognition and transferability of credits

New types of education providers, new delivery modes, new cross border education initiatives, new levels of student mobility, new opportunities for trade in higher education- all this can spell further confusion for the recognition of qualifications and transfer of academic credits. This is not a new issue. Trade agreements are not responsible for increased confusion, but they add to the complexity and also make resolution more urgent. National and international recognition of qualifications and the transfer of credits have already been the subject of a substantial amount of work. The 'Lisbon Convention on the Recognition of Qualifications of Higher Education in the Europe Region', the 'European Credit Transfer

System', and 'University Mobility in Asia Pacific' are good examples of regional initiatives that could lead to a more international approach.

Quality assurance and accreditation

Increased cross border education delivery and a set of legal rules and obligations in trade agreements require that urgent attention be given to the question of quality assurance and accreditation of education providers. Not only is it important to have national mechanisms which have the capacity to address accreditation and quality assessment procedures for the academic programs of new private and foreign providers, it is equally important that attention be given to developing an international approach to quality assurance and accreditation.

There is growing awareness that in the world of cross border education trade, national quality assurance schemes are becoming challenged by the complexities of the international education environment. While there may be growing awareness, there is no acceptance or agreement that harmonization of national policies with an international approach to quality assessment and accreditation is needed. It is imperative that education specialists discuss and determine the appropriate regulating mechanisms at the national and international level and not leave these questions to the designers and arbitrators of trade agreements.

Another, potentially contentious issue is the application of quality assurance schemes to both domestic and foreign providers. It may well be that under certain conditions, the national treatment obligation requires that all providers, domestic and foreign, be subject to the same processes and criteria. In some countries this will not be a problem, in others it will be hotly debated. Quality assurance of higher education in some countries is regulated by the sector, and in others by the government to a greater or lesser degree.

The key point is that authority for quality assurance, regulation and accreditation of cross border delivery needs to be examined and guided by stakeholders and bodies related to the education sector and not left solely in the hands of the market.

Research and intellectual property rights

In the new economy that emphasizes knowledge production and trade, there is increasingly more value attributed to the creative and intellectual content inherent in both products and services. The 'Trade-Related Aspects of Intellectual Property Rights' (TRIPS) is another trade agreement, completely separate from the GATS, but which also addresses trade liberalization. TRIPS covers such things as patents, trademarks and copyright, all of which are salient to the research and teaching/learning functions of higher education. Careful monitoring of TRIPS is also necessary by the higher education sector.

A look at the potential implications of trade agreements on research and scholarly work reveals a number of issues. A consistent theme expressed by trade critics is a deep concern about the increased emphasis on commercialization and commodification of the production of knowledge. Sceptics believe that the highly valued trinity of teaching, research and service at traditional universities may be at risk. A more differentiated and niche oriented approach to higher education may be an unanticipated outcome of increased trade in education and the growing importance of agreements such as GATS and TRIPS.

Internationalization

Attention needs to be given to the impact of trade liberalization on non-profit internationalization activities. Will trade overshadow and dominate the international academic relations of countries and institutions, or enhance them? Many internationalization strategies might be jeopardized by a purely commercial approach. For example, participation in international development or technical assistance programs can lead to mutual benefits for all partners and important spin-off effects for research, curriculum development and teaching.

Will these programs have less or more importance when there is increased pressure for trade? Will revenue raised from commercial education activities be used to subsidize internationalization activities? What might happen to student exchange, internships, and other forms of academic mobility that do not have an income generation or for-profit motive? Will limited financial resources be directed to trade initiatives that have an economic return instead of internationalization activities which stress added academic value?

How can internationalization and trade activities complement each other? Will bilateral relationships and multilateral networks among institutions be shaped by trade opportunities at the expense of research, curriculum development and other academic endeavours? Effort is needed to profile the benefits and importance of non-profit internationalization and to direct resources to the implementation and sustainability of the international dimension of teaching, research and service.

Mobility of Professionals/ Labour Force

It has already been noted that the GATS may address the widespread unmet demand for skilled workers by facilitating the mobility of professionals. This impacts many of the service sectors and has particular implications for higher education. Not only is higher and adult education providing education and training programs to meet economic needs, the sector itself is affected by the mobility of its teachers and researchers. In many countries, the increasing shortage of teachers is resulting in active recruitment campaigns across borders. Since many teachers and researchers want to move to countries with more favourable working conditions and salaries, there is a real concern that the most developed countries will benefit disproportionately.

Culture and Acculturation

Last, but certainly not least, is the issue of cultural and indigenous traditions. Education is a process through which cultural assimilation takes place. In fact education is a fundamental vehicle for acculturation. Concern about the homogenization of culture through cross border supply of higher and adult education is expressed by critics of GATS. Advocates maintain that a positive hybridization and fusion of culture will evolve through increasing mobility and the influence of ICTs. In fact, some argue that this has been happening for decades and is contributing to new cultural exchanges and richness. Once again, the divergence of opinion shows that there are potential opportunities and threats to consider.

Institutional Level Issues

The emphasis of this section has been on macro policy issues. But the effect on individual institutions, \especially public higher education institutions, should not be ignored. The foremost issues are institutional autonomy, academic freedom and conditions of employment for academic staff. While these three issues are linked to trade liberalization, they are more closely associated with the larger issues of the commercialization and privatization of education in general, which many believe is advanced within as well as across borders.

Trade Dominates

Finally, it needs to be said that the question of trade liberalization, which most often is interpreted in economic terms, has the potential of dominating the agenda. There is a risk of 'trade creep' where education policy issues are increasingly framed in terms of trade. Even though domestic challenges in education provision are currently front and centre on the radar screen of most countries, the issue of international trade in education services will most likely increase in importance.

Supporters of freer trade applaud the fact that GATS is seen first and foremost as an economic agreement and that its purpose is to promote and expand free trade for economic reasons. Given that the market potential for trade in higher education is already significant and is predicted to increase, it is clear that GATS and other trade agreements will help to promote trade and further economic benefit. Critics of the trade agreements maintain that the domination of the trade agenda is at the expense of other key objectives and rationales for higher education such as social, cultural and scientific development and the role of education in promoting democracy and citizenship.

Moving Foreword

Actions and reactions of stakeholders. One of the prime objectives of this report is to get the issue of trade liberalization in higher education services on the agenda of university managers and higher education policy makers. Overall, there seems to have been little reaction to the issue. This does not dismiss, however, the work that has been done by some non-government organizations.

One of the more interesting initiatives is the 'Joint Declaration on Higher Education and the General Agreement on Trade in Services' developed and signed by four organizations: Association of Universities and Colleges of Canada (AUCC), American Council on Education (ACE), European University Association (EUA) and the Council for Higher education Accreditation (CHEA).

This declaration encourages countries to not make commitments in 'Higher Education Services' or in the related categories of 'Adult Education' and 'Other Education Services' in the GATS. Instead it supports the notion of reducing obstacles to international trade in higher education using conventions and agreements outside of a trade policy regime. Clearly there are supporters of the principles of the declaration, but there are also critics who feel that the protectionist position is rather self-serving, especially given the degree of exporting activity already in existence.

It is noteworthy that three of the signatories come from the USA and Europe, both of whom have made some commitments on education services in GATS. This is yet another sign of the heated debate, the complexities and the uncertainties related to GATS.

The most important role of the declaration is that it is drawing more attention to the issue. The declaration is the only internationally co-ordinated effort but there are many national level student, teacher and education organizations that are vocal in their questions and criticisms of the intent and impact of the agreement.

There are similar groups such as the 'National Committee for International trade in Education' (NCITE) in the US and other business organizations which are expressing support for freer trade in education services. At the intergovernmental level there appears to be some level of interest in the issues - primarily from the economic organizations such as APEC or OECD. At the same time, there are international non-government organizations such as Association of Commonwealth Universities that are trying to raise awareness about the broad issue of trade liberalization and the specifics of the GATS. But, this is only a beginning.

More work is needed to consult with the different education stakeholders so that their voices are heard in ongoing analysis and negotiations.

Important dates for WTO negotiations

The key dates to be aware of for the next phases of the GATS negotiations are:

— *June 30, 2002:* Countries will file initial requests asking trading partners to open their markets in service areas.

— *March 31, 2003*: Countries that were the subjects of requests will present offers too pen their markets in service areas. Trading partners will hold meetings and discussions. Overall, if insufficient agreement is reached regarding higher education. The sector could be part of new round of global negotiations after talks conclude in January 2005.

— *January 2005:* GATS negotiations will end.

This is a rather tight timetable and the next twelve months are key. By June 2002, the details of all education requests should be known. While it is important that the voice of the education sector is heard in the formulation of these requests, it may be even more important to influence the response to the requests. This involves working with the appropriate government officials and monitoring the offers made by one's own country in response to requests from other countries.

The second part is monitoring the offers that are being received by one's own country in response to the requests originally made to other countries. This is an important, but a rather daunting task due to the reality that education stakeholders hold differing perspectives on the extent and nature of the limitations on national treatment and market access and may or may not speak with one voice to government trade officials.

Complex and contentious. These two words sum up the current analysis and debate about the impact of GATS on higher education. Opinions on the risks and benefits are divided, if not polarized. They differ within and between countries.

Each country must undertake the very serious challenge of balancing opportunities and commitments to liberalize trade for exporting higher education services, with the possible impact, related to the same commitments, of the import of education services. This is not an easy task.

One can tend to be liberal while considering exporting opportunities and more protection is when analysing the implications of importing. At this stage, one is left with the impression that there are more questions than clear answers. The questions are complex as they deal with:

— technical/legal issues of the agreement itself

— education policy issues such as funding, access, accreditation, quality and intellectual property and,·

— the larger more political/moral issues for society, such as the role and purpose of higher education, and the 'public good' or 'market commodity' approach.

The one certainty in this picture is the need for the higher education sector to study these questions and to consult stakeholders. At the same time it is necessary to be proactive and strategic in monitoring and influencing government negotiating positions for the request/offer stage of the GATS negotiations. This, of course, involves close communication with education departments and bodies in one's country. It is equally important not to lose sight of the need for international approaches and frameworks for the regulation of providers, quality assurance and qualification recognition. Finally, it is important not too ver state the impact of GATS. Trade in education was alive and well prior to and outside the purview of trade agreements. Yet, it is also critical not to understate the potential implications- risks and opportunities of GATS.

3

Education in a Knowledge Society

Two of the most important influences on educational planning today are what for want of an established name call all the futuristic business literature and the work coming out of cognitive science, broadly defined. There are, of course, many other influences, often from groups with a concern for some particular subject or aspect of schooling. But the two named are especially sweeping in their implications for educational change, each, in quite different ways, suggesting a reconceptualization of what schooling should be about. Yet each of these stops short of answering the question," What should it mean to be an educated person in the 21st century?" That is the kind of question that has motivated the development of liberal education and its periodic transformations.

The rise of the natural sciences led to the most profound transformation of liberal education. There were fears that it might not survive the transformation but it did, and no one would any longer conceive of an educated person who was ignorant of science. Now we are facing the possibility of a more radical transformation, one that does not involve so much the incorporation of new disciplines as a change in the way all disciplines are approached. Rumblings of such a transformation have been occurring throughout the past century, but the two new influences, along with the technologies they draw upon, may finally make it happen. Will it mean the end of liberal education or will liberal education re-emerge, strengthened through its renovation? Liberal education can be renewed, but it will take a careful synthesis of new ideas and enduring principles.

Liberal education is essentially enculturation. It is more than the handing on of a body of knowledge and wisdom, although that is a large part of it. That is the part that liberal education has in common with enculturation in all societies. What makes liberal education distinctive -what makes it 'liberal'-is its cosmopolitanism. Liberal education initiates the young into a culture that transcends the particularities of their social and ethnic backgrounds. A major concern of many advocates of liberal education is that cosmopolitanism itself is coming under attack. It has been more than adequately discussed. Instead, assume in the ensuing discussion that cosmopolitanism of some kind is an agreed-upon end of education. The liberal tradition, the new wave of economic globalization, and recent advances in the learning sciences all point in this direction. But how is such cosmopolitanism to be achieved when cultures are colliding and undergoing rapid, perhaps catastrophic change, when knowledge is expanding more rapidly than anyone can keep up with, and when the process of enculturation itself is subject to radical innovation?

The discussion begins by drawing out the contrasting educational implications of the futuristic business literature and of cognitive learning research the one emphasizing skills and personal qualities, the other emphasizing knowledge. Merging the two into lists of educational objectives, as is now common, does not begin to resolve underlying differences. The resolution propose depends upon taking seriously the idea of a knowledge society, a society organized around the production of knowledge in the same sense that an agrarian society is organized around agricultural production and an industrial society is organized around manufacture. The school should be a productive part of that society, a workshop for the generation of knowledge. Transforming schools into workshops for the production of knowledge mobilizes those skills and personal qualities valued by business futurists, putting them to work toward ends that are consistent with contemporary conceptions of learning and with the objectives of a modernized liberal education.

Two Views of Education for the 21st Century

By the 'futuristic business literature' refer to that flood of publications from organizational theorists, management consultants, economists, futurologists, and diverse social scientists that take as a backdrop the rapid rate of technological change, the rise of Asia Pacific economies, digitization, globalization, outsourcing, the shift from a manufacturing-based to a knowledge-based economy, and the need for constant innovation. This literature covers a great range in quality of ideas, which raises the twin dangers that policy makers may be influenced most by the lowest level and easiest to grasp ideas and that discriminating people will reject the whole literature, thereby ignoring ideas that provide a basis for well-reasoned new educational policies.

Some low-end educational ideas are that technology will revolutionize everything, that we don't need schools anymore, and that there is no use mastering any body of knowledge because it will soon be obsolete. The high-end educational ideas mainly flow from a recognition of the ascendant importance of knowledge: knowledge as a third factor in production, along with capital and labor; learning as the means for organizations to gain a competitive edge; finally, the idea of a social transformation going on that is as extreme as the 19th-century shift from an agrarian to an industrial society the shift to a knowledge society.

When it comes to formulating curriculum guidelines, however, the low-end and the high-end ideas seem to point in the same direction. They point to a set of personal qualities that must be cultivated if the education system is to produce people who can thrive in and contribute to the new order: imagination and creativity, ability to work in groups, communication skills, information-finding skills, problem solving abilities, technological literacy, and above all a continual readiness to learn. It is difficult to fault these, and they are now appearing conspicuously in curriculum guidelines and standards. But are they sufficient, and do they point educational planning in the right direction?

Cognitive science embraces an increasing range of approaches, addressing an increasing range of issues. It gains its strength from disciplined pursuit of the question," How does it work?" Cognitive learning research shares this wide-open character. There is no established 'cognitive approach' in education. Yet, for all its diversity, when the work of cognitive educational researchers is put alongside the futuristic business literature, the kinds of prescriptions for education in the 21st century suggested by these two bodies of work are seen to differ profoundly. The emphasis of the business literature is on process outcomes, on turning out students who function in such-and-such ways.

The current emphasis in cognitive learning research is on content, on turning out students with a genuine understanding of science, mathematics, and other school subjects. Educational reformers inspired by the futuristic business literature commonly minimize the value of content mastery. For instance, an announcement of Stanford University's "Just-In-Time Learning on Internet " project confidently proclaims," Traditional text books and traditional teaching methods requiring weeks of study are being made obsolete by the information explosion." The project leaders suggest that publishers might abandon their traditional bookish ways and start charging customers on a "pay-per-question" basis.

Are cognitive learning researchers, then, simply out of touch with the digital age? On the contrary, it seems that most of the business writers along with many educators, unfortunately are out of touch with progress in the understanding of learning. In the 1970s, cognitive learning research was where the futuristic literature is now, emphasizing cognitive strategies and learning-to-learn. For a combination of reasons, the emphasis has since shifted dramatically toward content learning. First there was the research on reading, which demonstrated that the overriding determinant of what one will get out of reading is what one already knows about the topic.

Then there was the accumulation of research on expertise, which showed that in all kinds of areas, practical as well as intellectual, expertise depends more on deep knowledge of one's domain, its problems and tools, than it does on general mental abilities. Perhaps most surprising was the research on misconceptions, which added up to the conclusion that students are passing through the schools having failed to grasp most of the ideas that constitute modern knowledge. Schools, it appears, are turning out graduates with pre Newtonian conceptions of physics, preDarwinian conceptions of biology, and preSmithian conceptions of economics. This ought at least to give some pause to futurists who imagine students at home in a postmodern world of quanta and dynamic systems.

Finally, however, the emphasis on content has been buoyed by the successes of new educational efforts aimed at learning with understanding. Once students start to get deeply into the pursuit of understanding, they begin to show spontaneously all the traits that the futuristic business literature urges: imagination, collaboration, problem-solving, communicative skill, and readiness to go on learning. A commonsense response to the differing implications of futuristic business literature and cognitive learning research would be," Let's have both". Why not teach both the general skills and dispositions urged by the former and the deep content knowledge stressed by the latter? In fact, that is what curriculum guidelines and standards are tending increasingly to propose. Attractive as this eclectic solution may be, its effect is to drain away the energy that might have produced something new and exciting out of the interaction of these two new forces.

A New Culture for Learning

The futuristic business literature does convey a revolutionary vision, but it is not to be found in the paragraphs on education. Those are, for the most part, a mixture of technological euphoria and run-of-the-mill school-bashing. The revolutionary vision has to do with knowledge-based organizations ones whose competitive advantage depends on cultivation and use of the organization's knowledge resources. Because those knowledge resources are generated out of (and to a large extent reside in) the work of everyone in the organization, maximizing them requires designing the organization so as to make everyone a contributor. That is the revolutionary part: abandoning bureaucratic structures in which a worker's responsibility is defined by routine tasks and where non routine problems are referred to a higher level, replacing them by mission-oriented team structures in which problems are solved and new knowledge is generated within the working groups. That vision has much in common with a new vision of education taking shape within cognitive learning research.

Early cognitive learning research was not only focused on cognitive strategies, it was also focused on the individual learner. Along with a shift toward content came a shift from trying to inculcate learning strategies in the individual student to trying to create classroom cultures that support inquiry and the pursuit of deeper understanding. Educational historians will probably give credit for this shift to a revival of Vygotsky's socio-cultural theory of development and to the theory of situated cognition, which came out of anthropology. These ideas found a ready audience, however, among cognitive learning researchers who had spent the previous decade trying to improve learning by teaching individual cognitive strategies, it was not that the strategies did not work or that they were too hard to teach. The results were often quite impressive in the short run. We seemed to be teaching a level of mental activity beyond anything required in normal schooling. It became evident, therefore, that any general upgrading of students' intellectual abilities and dispositions would require changing the prevailing culture of the classroom. Ordinary classroom life is organized around activities. This is true across the whole spectrum ranging from tightly controlled classrooms where the main activity is filling in workbook pages to child-centered classrooms where the activities are self-chosen and often self-initiated projects.

The new challenge has become to reorganize classroom life around the pursuit of knowledge. The shift from focus on individual cognitive strategies to classroom culture is clearly delineated in the influential work of Ann Brown. In the 1970s her research dealt with teaching memory strategies to mildly retarded children. By the 1980s individual strategy instruction had evolved into 'reciprocal teaching', in which children were organized into what might be characterized as rather highly structured support groups for reading comprehension. Reciprocal teaching then became assimilated into the more comprehensive 'communities of learners' in which the students became researchers and teachers of one another. Similar if not so clearly demarcated shifts occurred among many of the other cognitive learning researchers who had started out working with individual cognitive strategies.

The cultural shift that is implied in the new cognitive approaches remains poorly understood in the educational community, however the shift, that is, from classroom life organized around activities to classroom life organized around the pursuit of knowledge. Instead, reciprocal teaching, communities of learners, and other transformations of classroom culture are merely perceived as new activities to replace supplement old ones. The hottest innovations going in schooling today are 'project-based learning' and 'multiple intelligences.' The first is an old idea from the progressive education era brought back to life by new electronic media. The second is based on a theory of intelligence that has stimulated the invention of all kinds of new activities. New and more educative activities may indeed improve learning, but they short-circuit efforts to bring about the cultural shift that seems essential if schools are to play the role in knowledge development that cognitive research indicates they should.

This cultural shift must assume a more revolutionary form. Otherwise it will be continually reduced to "hands-on learning," "learner-centered education," or some other refurbishment of progressive education. Here is where the ideas about organizational transformation and knowledge work, prominent in the business literature, may be of service. Schools be reconstituted along the lines of other organizations whose function is to produce knowledge. Learning goes on in all organizations, but only some organizations have the function of producing knowledge. The learning that goes on in any organization, whether it is a shoe factory or a research laboratory, is internal to individual minds and to the developing practices of work groups and of the organization as a whole.

The excitement over the idea of a 'learning organization' reflects a growing appreciation of the value of this learning. It increases the competence of the organization to perform its functions; in these intensely competitive times, learning is one way for an organization to gain a competitive edge. Accordingly, we see efforts to promote learning that range from formal courses in company-run schools to coffee bars where employees may hang out and exchange instructive stories about their work. In addition, however, and quite apart from this internal betterment that we call learning, some organizations have the job of producing knowledge.

These include university research centers, independent laboratories, market research and opinion research companies, and research and design departments within larger organizations. Unfortunately, in the current learning organization lingo, this knowledge production is called learning, too, thus obscuring an important distinction. Of course, learning goes on in these knowledge-producing organizations as in all others -learning that develops the competence of the organization to do its work. But the work of the organization is not learning. It is producing knowledge. We accordingly refer to these as knowledge building organizations.

A research laboratory is a knowledge-building organization. A shoe factory is not, although it may contain a research group that is. Schools today are not knowledge building organizations. That is a radical cultural shift. The school becomes a workshop for the production of knowledge. The students are workers. They are learners, too, of course; and because of the nature of their work they may be expected to learn a great deal. But learning is not their job. Their job is producing knowledge. It is meaningful work, because what they are producing is something for their own use, and so their work has that quality, so rare in the industrial age, that comes with building one's own house or raising one's own food.

Many educators would endorse this proposal in the belief that it is what they are already doing. Yet very little of so-called 'constructivist' pedagogy that have observed or read about is actually concerned with the production of knowledge. Instead, it is concerned with the carrying out of projects that use knowledge but have some other objective than its production. Students may plan a trip to Mars or the building of a station on the moon, they may draw up an environmental or a business plan, or they may play a game or even create a game. At their best, such projects may generate a considerable amount of learning, but it is important to realize the difference between them and authentic knowledge creation.

In the course of studying ocean habitats, elementary school students were set to work creating educational computer games related to the ocean theme. Community of Learners and CSILE as 'project-based' approaches. While that is an accurate categorization, it reflects the common weakness in elementary education for elevating a procedural characteristic to the status of a pedagogical philosophy. The authors then proceed to distinguish Learning Science Through Design from the other two approaches in that it is less structured and awards students a higher level of "creative control over the production of an artifact." Evidently the students did throw themselves energetically into creating the computer games; they collaborated, consulted experts, and discussed programming problems. So if the purpose was to teach software design and programming, the project would have to be considered a success.

A computer bulletin board was used for discussion, but, the discussions were about game design and programming, not about oceans. Incredibly, the one science question posted was rejected by the teacher, who told the student not to expect others to do his research for him! The authors are candid in concluding that "Learning Science Through Design "in this instance failed "to create a consistent context for a deeper level of subject inquiry," and they suggest that in the future their method might need" to structure the electronic exchanges around content more along the lines described by both Scardamalia and her colleagues in the CSILE project and Brown and her colleagues in the COL environment." This sounds like a minor modification in procedure, however, whereas doing so successfully that is, getting students truly engaged with problems of marine biology instead of being solely concerned with software design would involve a shift in focus so radical that the game-building activity might no longer be relevant.

Students in a Community of Learners classroom intensely engaged with the problem of how male sea otters are able to mark off a territory of clean as their own a problem that was not handed to them but that they hit upon themselves as an anomaly in information they had assembled. The same sort of thing occurred in a CSILE classroom when a group studying the Arctic biome could not reconcile the reasons they were given for why trees do not grow in the Arctic with information other groups were providing about trees growing in deserts and in tropical rainforests. The issue here is not only the learning of science content. It is also learning about knowledge: learning that it is more than stuff sitting in textbooks to be used for answering quiz questions. Even more, it is a matter of gaining experience of what take to be the essence of life in a knowledge building organization the experience of producing knowledge of real value to someone.

But the extreme prominence given to them in modern pedagogy suggests to me an underlying belief that students have to be lured into learning, that they cannot be expected to pursue knowledge in its own right. No one says this openly, however, for belief in children's natural curiosity as the driving force in learning is one of the pillars of child-centered education.

However, is something even less savory. Educators examples of students 'genuine, sustained efforts to construct real knowledge, someone almost always remarks," That's fine for students who are motivated, but what about..." and there follows one of those shrugs or evasive mumbles that are meant to convey that we all know what kind of kids we are talking about although it is no longer safe to label them. The unrealistic part of the child-centered faith is the belief that each child's natural curiosity should be sufficient to sustain knowledge-seeking six or more hours a day for 12 or more years. Those of us who are trying to change classroom culture are not banking on that. Rather, the expectation is that if the production of usable knowledge gets established as the classroom's collective task, then ordinary motives of conformity and citizenship will suffice to keep students engaged when curiosity flags. There may be situations where establishing the classroom as a knowledge production workshop proves impossible, but it is certainly a more attainable objective than keeping the curiosity of 30 individual students constantly aroused.

Knowledge Construction in the Classroom

The idea of schools as workshops for the construction of knowledge wins ready assent from educators. The difficulty is in getting them to see that this is anything different from students planning space missions: It is all "project-based learning" or playing at being scientists. In discussing adult organizations earlier, it was easy to distinguish learning from knowledge building. Everyone learns, and progressive organizations do much to promote learning, but learning is not what people are employed for. Creating or adding value to knowledge, by constrast, is the purpose of an increasing number of jobs. Learning is the reason we send children to school, however, and knowledge building is only going to be valued insofar as students learn from doing it. But that does not make the distinction between learning and knowledge building any the less important. Students currently engage in all kinds of schoolwork, from doing sheets of arithmetic exercises to producing elaborate multimedia presentations, most of which is far removed from any kind of work that goes on in a knowledge society.

Since students need to do some kind of work in order to learn, why not let that work be the construction of knowledge. The reason we need a distinction between learning and knowledge building is in order for a statement like that to make sense. One major prejudice must be overcome if knowledge building, as real productive work similar to what goes on in industrial laboratories and university research centers, is to find a foothold in educational policy. This is the prejudice that bestows credit only on the first person to come forth with an idea. Although this may be a perfectly reasonable principle in patent law, when generalized it virtually denies the possibility of children's being real creators of knowledge; for rarely if ever will a child produce knowledge that is new to the world. But originality is always relative to context. If it should turn out that there are intelligent beings on another planet and that everything scientists on earth have discovered is already old hat to them, would that mean that Newton and Darwin were not scientists after all?

Furthermore, an original theory or explanation is only one kind of knowledge product, albeit an exceptionally important one. Other worthwhile products of knowledge building are interpretations of theories, criticisms, translations of them into simpler terms, analyses of their implications or applications in some context of interest, descriptions of phenomema which the theory does or does not explain, experimental demonstrations, simulations, and historical accounts. Many adults pursue respectable careers producing knowledge of these kinds, often demonstrating creativity and depth of insight in the process. There is no reason to deny students credit when they do likewise.

A student in a CSILE class enters a note asking what keeps gravity from leaving the earth. Later another student, she has read that gravity is a force between things and therefore not something contained within things. Several students seize on this as making sense of the idea they have heard that gravity is everywhere. As we adults read these notes we conclude that a genuine advance in knowledge has occurred, helped along as much by the first student's naive question as by the second student's important finding. We do not know how much has been learned that is, how much individual students in the class will carry away from this episode. Undoubtedly it will vary. What we do know is that knowledge has been produced, not of news-making or prize-winning calibre, but as important to the intellectual world that the students live in as the discoveries of a leading-edge university research team are to the intellectual world they live in. That is really all we need to allow in order to accept knowledge building by students as genuine productive work rather than merely a learning activity.

The preceding example combines remarks made by various students when asked to tell about their class's work. It is very similar to what one might get on dropping in on a university research group and asking how their work was going. The knowledge that the students have constructed is of course of a different order, but their unsolved problems are indeed unsolved in the world at large. They can legitimately claim membership in the communities of people who are working on such problems. They are, in short, doing real knowledge building, not playing pretend. Over the span of the school years, the job of students in the knowledge workshop is to construct an understanding of the whole world. Only today's students may go at it with more help and with improved tools and resources.

The achievement of such a unified and comprehensive understanding has traditionally been the highest aim of liberal education. However, in the past it has been seen as largely a matter of gaining possession of an existing understanding of the known world, such as Aristotle's or those of the medieval Summae or later the enlightenment project of Diderot's Encyclopedie. There were, of course, students who went beyond these fixed understandings to construct knowledge of their own, but in doing so they went well beyond the expectations of the curriculum and perhaps even beyond its allowable limits. The proposal to make knowledge building the principal activity in schooling would mean enlarging liberal education so as to encompass both the grasping of what others have already understood and the sustained, collective effort to extend the boundaries of what is known.

Multiculturalists, Marxist critics, and advocates of liberal education are alike in regarding schooling as a form of enculturation. "What should it mean to be an educated person in the 21st century?" we have to consider what kind of culture is foreseen and how schooling should relate to it. There is much more to this issue. The uncertainties of prediction and the alarming nature of many trends in contemporary culture are daunting. One social prediction seems much less risky than others, however, and that is the expectation of a continuing rise in the importance of knowledge and knowledge work. The only way this prediction could prove wrong would be if knowledge and technology stopped advancing, and barring worldwide suppression that could not occur. We do not know what the social consequences will be for employment, equity, quality of life, and so on -no matter how confidently pundits may extrapolate current trends. What we can say is that knowledge will be an increasingly salient part of the environment. You will not know your way around in tomorrow's world unless you know your way around knowledge.

A statement like the preceding can, however, mean next to nothing in a discussion of educational policy. To many people these days it will mean knowing your way around on the Internet, knowing how to do searches for Worldwide Web documents. The Web does, in fact, nicely epitomize a world overrun with knowledge; and so amazed to keep encountering writers on the Web proclaiming the centrality of information search skills as an educational objective for the knowledge age. The skills needed to do web searches can be learned in a few hours (less, if you know a bit of Boolean algebra). But years of subject-matter learning must come to the fore if you are to avoid retrieving thousands of documents none of which contains the information you were hoping to find.

Knowing around the Worldwide Web really means being on familiar terms with world knowledge in its manifold aspects. The more you know the greater your chance of learning something new. That is the real excitement of the new knowledge resources, yet it seems scarcely to be appreciated at all by the information media enthusiasts presuming to lead? education into the knowledge age. If it were appreciated, it would go some way toward re-establishing the importance of liberal education. The trouble, lies in a folk psychology which conceives of the mind as a storehouse of items of information, along with a set of mental abilities and skills for working with those items.

With this conception, it is very difficult to think of knowledge as the principal basis for finding or acquiring new knowledge, just as it is difficult to think of knowledge production as distinct from learning. We need a broader conception of knowledge. We must be able to treat it as a part of the world -along with computers, CD players, backpacks, and street people that students become enculturated into. Without that, schooling will remain lodged in an earlier and more primitive age, no matter how many computers line the walls, and will little prepare students for the world that exists on the other side of the modem. Working out a vision for education in a knowledge society minimally requires taking account of knowledge in two quite distinct senses: first, knowledge as something that people acquire and that becomes a part of them; second, knowledge as something that they work with and that in some sense takes in a life of its own.

The knowledge building classroom, as characterizing it, embodies this dual conception of knowledge. It thus presents a miniature of the knowledge society into which students are to become enculturated. Common sense of course recognizes this dual character of knowledge. When we talk about a child 'knowing (or not knowing) the Pythagorean theorem 'we simultaneously refer to knowledge as an attribute of the child's mental state and to the Pythagorean theorem as a piece of knowledge in its own right -as something created by a mathematician in ancient times and surviving to this day as a worthwhile thing-to-be-known. But in order to carry on a serious discussion about knowledge in education, we need distinguishing labels. Which can be quite useful so long as we are careful not to encumber them with excess meaning. The labels come from his metaphor of three worlds. World 1, the physical world, need not concern us at this point.

The important distinction is between Worlds 2 and 3. World 2 is the subjective world, comprising the knowledge in people's heads. (Without doing violence to Popper's concept, we can expand World 2 to include situated knowledge as well knowledge that is implicit in the practices of communities and not assignable to individual minds.) World 3 is, roughly speaking, the world of ideas. It consists of immaterial knowledge objects that can be discussed, modified, replaced, and so on.

The Pythagorean theorem is an object in World 1, the child's knowledge of the Pythagorean theorem is part of the child's World 1, the distinction thus coincides with the distinction have been making between knowledge building and learning. Knowledge building is work carried out to produce changes in World 3. Learning consists of changes in World 2. From an educational standpoint, what is especially attractive about the World 3 idea is that it encompasses both the traditional idea of a fund of accumulated knowledge that is passed on to the young and the more dynamic idea of knowledge advancing through people's creative efforts. We may think of World 3 as a workspace in which there are knowledge objects in various stages of development.

Some are finished to the extent that no one bothers to tinker with them anymore. Some, like phlogiston theory, are of no current value and are preserved for historical interest only. Others are under current development and are the subjects of research, criticism, controversy, repair operations, and novel conjecture. The Pythagorean theorem is one of the finished objects of World 3. But when students produce explanations of the theorem or intuitive proofs or examples of application, these are World 3 objects as well and the activity that produces them is work in World 3, just as was the work of Pythagoras. This conception of World 3 as a realm of activity stretches Popper's concept, but not very much.

Translating it into an educational prescription leads naturally to thinking of World 3 as a workspace and of education as providing entree to it. Accordingly, we may define the role of schools in the knowledge age as follows: It is to enculturate students into World 3. Enculturation into World 3 entails much more than mastering a body of established knowledge. Indeed, it leaves open such questions as what constitutes established knowledge and what needs to be mastered and in what ways. It implies, rather, that those perennial curriculum issues should be considered within the context of students' active participation in the world where such issues matter.

Enculturation into any world means becoming familiar with what is there, learning how to act, becoming involved in what is going on, and generally coming to feel at home in it. At a deeper level, enculturation implies that artifacts and activities will come to have a meaning for the newcomer that is consistent with the meaning they have for others in that world. This does not mean that one becomes the same as everyone else, but it does mean that the world is no longer exotic, bewildering, or forbidding.

In short, a whole epistemology is represented here, an epistemology sophisticated enough for the knowledge age and something far beyond what educators speak of as 'cooperative learning,'' problem-based learning,' 'constructivist learning,' or ((groan)' learner-centered education.' It is knowledge-centered education; and Mendel gets into the picture, not as a dead white male with the authority of the scientific establishment behind him but as someone with a contribution to make to a current knowledge problem. For Popper, as a philosopher of science, World 3 consisted primarily of discussible propositions or declarative knowledge—theories, conjectures, problem formulations, historical accounts, interpretations, proofs, criticisms, and the like.

However, he saw these as cultural objects existing in a larger world that includes other cultural objects such as poems, sonatas, folktales, food recipes, rituals, and monuments. Liberal education is enculturation into this larger world of cultural objects. World 3 is and always has been an important part of the world for liberal education. The world of cultural objects is quite different for a liberally educated Indonesian, for instance, from what it is for a liberally educated Italian. To be sure, both would probably score better on a test of cultural literacy than would the average American student for whom it was designed; but in the art, literature, music, and history with which they are intimately familiar, there will be profound differences.

These differences are valuable; cultures are kept alive by people who cherish and live on intimate terms with the objects of their cultures, and this is much of what gives richness to life. But it is important to recognize that things are different with the objects of World 3. Multiculturalists to the contrary, there are not culture-specific sciences, mathematics, literary or historical theories.

There are cultural differences, just as there are individual differences, in how people think about these things; but they are not differences that preclude constructive criticism and collaborative knowledge building. Or if they are, then something is wrong that education needs to set right. The boundaries of World 3 are approximately the boundaries of what can be profitably argued about in general terms. Liberal education, has the dual task of expanding those boundaries and of equipping students to engage in the argument. Not that arguing is all one does with World 3 objects; there is finding implications and applications, explaining, comparing, revising, and so on. But if a proposition is not arguable it is generally not amenable to these other operations either, and if people do not understand a World 3 object well enough to argue constructively about it they are probably not competent to do much else with it.

Liberal education today is embroiled in serious controversy about what cultural objects, representing whose culture, are to figure in the curriculum. This is an important controversy, accentuated by the increasing cultural divisions to be found within modern societies. But the largest cultural divide, cutting across the whole world with great consequence, is that which separates people who are at home in World 3 from those who are not. Any decision about enculturation that excludes students from enculturation into a cosmopolitan World 3 is a serious denial of children's rights to education.

Exclusion from World 3 could come in the form of an educational program so intent on preserving indigenous culture or ethnic pride that it relegates World 3 to the status of a foreign culture. This is what is happening when educators start referring to 'Eurocentric science,' for instance. Or exclusion could take the form of an educational program so child-centered or so intent on learning objectives that there is no participation in any larger intellectual world. Much of what is going on in education seems to be exclusionary in one or more of these ways. It seems that the education system itself is on the wrong side of the cultural divide, ill-disposed to treat knowledge as a focus of productive work. Better models of schooling are available, models that are compatible with the needs of a knowledge-based economy, with the best of cognitive learning research, and with enduring values of liberal education. Variations on project-based learning or whatever new method comes to the fore. In order to move to the other side of the divide, in order to find their place in a knowledge society, schools must undergo a much more radical transformation. Only by becoming knowledge building organizations themselves, can schools hope to provide students with a way into the life of a knowledge society.

4

Background of Multicultural Education

Cultures are the linguistic, religious, artistic, and mythological ways in which groups of the species *homo sapiens* express their originality. Of course, cultures can seem like stronger divisions than that: Cultural differences can become the fault lines in a society that offer pretenses for mistreatment, discrimination against, and oppression of one group by another.

Multicultural education came into being where fair-minded people sought ways to respond constructively to the challenge of members of different cultural groups sharing the same society. Although social action for justice may begin in other domains— laws and policies, hiring practices, housing, or access to health care, for example—sooner or later, schools must be involved in the effort. That is because progress in social arrangements ultimately requires that citizens adopt new attitudes, which in turn need new knowledge and experiences. A new education is needed by people on both sides of the cultural divide. Children of groups who have been oppressed need bolstering; and children of privileged groups need to broaden their perspective to take into account the views of children from other groups.

Multicultural education, then, is a movement in schools to promote awareness, mutual appreciation, and harmony among people of different cultural groups—usually with the ultimate goal of achieving social justice and social cohesion.

Those who pay serious attention to what happens in schools know that schooling has a formal and an informal side. On the formal or explicit side are the objectives of the state curriculum and the content of school books and lectures, as measured by examinations.

On the informal or hidden side are power relationships and implicit expectations for behavior: For example, do we succeed by cooperating or competing? Do students share responsibility for the classroom or only take orders? Also part of the informal side are attitudes toward one sex or one cultural group as opposed to another.

This aspect of the informal or hidden curriculum is often evidenced in what is *not* included in the formal curriculum: Whose pictures do not hang in the hallways, or are not seen in books? Whose stories are not told? Whose contributions to society are not chronicled?

Teachers who approach multicultural education often begin with the formal curriculum—with the content that is taught. Some, however, attempt to change the implicit aspects of schooling, too—to make aspects of schooling like power-sharing and interaction among students more supportive of students from all cultural groups and ultimately of the goal of social change.

A Model of Prejudice and Multicultural Education

Attitudes are not learned cognitively like facts and dates. How does multicultural education affect attitudes and outlooks toward cultures—one's own and others? The answer lies in the interaction between concepts and experience. Let us look, first, at how this interaction affects members of the dominant group.

> In their early years, members of Group Y begin to hear disparaging remarks said about members of Group X. They may hear these remarks, and detect the attitude they convey, before those members of Group Y have any real experience with members of Group X. The prejudicial remarks predispose them to have negative experiences with members of Group X when they eventually meet one: Members of Group Y will be willing to interpret virtually anything the Group X person says or does as evidence of their ________ or their _______ (whatever negative attribute they have learned to associate with members of that group). When that happens, they are now likely assume that our negative view of members of Group X is based on direct experience! They know that members of Group X have these negative attributes, because they have seen them with their own eyes!
>
> Unfortunately, this phenomenon may affect members of Group X as well, if all majority of the cultural reminders they see in public either ignore Group X—or worse, portray them in a negative light—members of Group X may, at best, conclude that they are not very important, that they don't really belong in the school or in the community; and at worst, that they really do possess the negative features that members of Group Y have ascribed to them.

These gloomy processes can be prevented from happening, however. Cognitive psychologists tell us, just as the model suggested, that we tend to notice what we know about: A person who knows her wild flowers will have an altogether different experience of a walk through a field than a person who knows nothing about wild flowers. Similarly, if in school, children from Group Y are taught many fascinating features of the culture of Group X, as well as many features that Group Y has in common with that group, then their personal experience with members of that group will no longer automatically lead them to form negative conclusions about them. Similarly, if members of Group X see people like themselves reflected in the school curriculum, and begin to see positive features and accomplishments of their group *validated in the school*, they will feel less alienated and more encouraged by their school experiences.

Both of the examples given above together have been called the *window and mirror* effects of multicultural education (Simms Bishop, 1996). Multicultural education provides a *window* into the cultures of minority children, through which children from majority groups can see them accurately. It also provides a *mirror* of their own culture, to children from minority groups, who heretofore may have seen only negative reflections of themselves, or no reflection at all, in the school curriculum.

Admittedly, a few widely scattered exercises in cultural awareness will not go very far to combat years of prejudicial attitudes that have been absorbed at home or in the neighborhood. That is why many experts in multicultural education argue for the infusion of multicultural influences throughout the curriculum and throughout the school day, week, and year. In fact, approaches that have been taken to multicultural education can be plotted along a continuum from occasional topic lessons to a transformation of the school.

Models of Multicultural Education

In the most straightforward of venues, multicultural education is limited to discussions of school curriculum. From a practical standpoint, this translates into using materials such as children's books, or projects such as oral histories, to increase awareness and understanding of the various cultural perspectives of the students in the school or classroom. The idea is that the content connects to the child and hence, each child will see himself or herself reflected in the daily curriculum and studies that take place in the classroom. Further, that the class will see itself as a collective made up of different experiences, all of which are equally important and valid, and by doing so will increase the understanding of each child of the other.

In other contexts, such as the political arena, multicultural education takes on a much broader scope and has been defined as "any set of processes by which schools work with rather than against oppressed groups." The most inclusive definitions suggest that multicultural education is a transformational process that permeates and impacts every aspect of the operation of an educational system, including government policy, staffing, curriculum, disciplinary policy, student involvement, parent and community involvement, pedagogy, assessment, and funding.

One of the underlying premises of multicultural education as transformation is "that as schools go so goes the nation," At the practical level, multicultural education then becomes a venue for social and political reform. Discussions of oppression, social inequality, power dynamics, race and ethnicity, as well as the role of the dominant culture, in the shaping of society's basic assumption about what constitutes school knowledge, appropriate social behavior, and national identity, is all part of the multicultural education discourse.

Regardless of where practice comes down on the definitional continuum, researchers, architects, and practitioners of multicultural education hold certain goals and assumptions in common.

Multicultural education assumes that pluralism is a good thing and that race, ethnicity, cultural and social class are all salient parts of a pluralistic society. Participation in a variety of ethnic experiences ultimately enriches one's understanding of the human experience and leads to a more fulfilling life.

A central goal of multicultural education is to help individuals live more productively in a pluralistic society. This is accomplished in two ways:

— Individuals gain a greater understanding of themselves by seeing themselves through the lens of other cultures.

— Individuals gain the necessary skills, knowledge, and attitudes needed to function within their ethnic culture and within and across other ethnic cultures.

Multicultural education is premised on the need for accuracy. In order for individuals to get a true picture of historical and social events, which have shaped national identity, they need to listen to multiple voices and understand multiple perspectives. It is not a matter of leaving out one version of events in favor of another; rather it is about re-envisioning history using an inclusive model that more accurately portrays events as they happened.

Multicultural education is a commitment to helping all students master the essential academic and social skills to become knowledgeable, caring, and active citizens in an increasingly polarized and troubled world.

Models of Multicultural Education Programs: Theory Into Practice

Regardless of how individuals view the multicultural education movement, there are some general models and specific areas of research that offer educators and policy makers a road map for program development. The two most often cited general modes are offered by Banks and by Sleeter and Gran These models differ from one another but are not mutually exclusive.

Other researchers such as Nieto, Delpit, and Ladson-Billings focus on particular areas of multicultural program development and offer suggestions relating to pedagogy, curriculum, and structure. Ladson-Billings, for example, focuses on the specifics of successful literacy education for African American students. Delpit is concerned with power relations in a classroom that can exist when minority children are taught by teachers of the dominant culture. Nieto is focused on institutional reform and student achievement.

When discussing theoretical models, how they actually look and operate in a classroom or school is often left out of the conversation. In that regard, Burnett suggests a third model that combines Banks, Sleeter, current research with an overview of actual programs as they are currently underway in the United States. Burnett's typology is particularly useful in that it reflects the translation of theory into practice and divides programs into three general categories according to program emphasis.

Content-Oriented Programs

Content-oriented programs are the most easily recognizable and hence the most common form of multicultural education. Content-oriented programs are committed to the inclusion of material that reflects the cultural make-up of the class or the school. The primary goal of these programs is to make students more knowledgeable about cultures within their schools or their communities.

Content-oriented programs come in various levels of engagement and infusion of the curriculum. In its simplest form, "this type of program gives a multicultural patina to the standard curriculum" by incorporating a few readings and the celebration of heroes and holidays of diverse groups. It gives only a cursory nod to multicultural education by focusing solely on "heroes and holiday." Students would read books, do projects, and learn about a variety of holidays but through the lens of the standard canon. At this stage, multicultural education is an add-on or tangential to current curriculum without changing the actual focus. More sophisticated and complex programs, however, set out to actually transform the curriculum. These programs have three goals:

- to develop multicultural content across the disciplines
- to incorporate a variety of different viewpoints and perspectives in the curriculum
- to transform the canon, ultimately developing a new paradigm for the curriculum

These programs can come in many forms, but often the most common is a single group study, such as women's studies, ethnic studies, etc. These programs can be the focus of the whole school, as in the examples of Afrocentric and single sex schools, or only portions of the curriculum.

Student-Oriented Programs

Student-oriented programs address the academic and learning needs of carefully defined groups of students, most specifically minority students. The goal of these programs is often to raise the academic achievement of these groups. Research in learning styles, language use and development, etc. often forms the basis of these programs.

Since the goal of student-oriented programs is to improve the academic success of specific groups and thereby make it possible for them to enter the mainstream, they are often seen as compensatory in nature. Further, there is no particular guarantee that student-oriented programs will be done in conjunction with content oriented programs. In fact, it is entirely possible to have one without the other. Again Banks suggests four broad program categories:

— programs that use research into culturally-based learning styles in order to match teaching styles to a specific group of students

— bi-lingual education or language/cultural immersion

— special math and science programs for groups, such as females and minorities that are seen as underachieving in these areas.

— Language programs and cultural programs specific to minority group

Socially-Oriented Programs

Socially-oriented programs are generally the most inclusive and broad-based. They are also often controversial and as a consequence less common. Programs such as these attempt to reform "both the schooling and the cultural and political contexts of schooling". The over-arching goal of socially-oriented programs is to increase cultural and racial tolerance and reduce bias as well as rearrange the social structure to reinforce and support this new paradigm.

In order to accomplish this, socially-oriented programs have a number of distinguishing characteristics:

— They seek to revise and transform the curriculum to create a new canon that is reflective of the current society.

— They seek to use current educational research to discover new ways to engage students in the educational enterprise in order that they may be academically successful, regardless of ethnicity and class.

— They use the instruments and strategies of social activism and community organization to accomplish these goals.

— They focus on the outcome of preparing students to be socially - active citizens and agents of change.

Sleeter and Grant have described socially-oriented programs as about human relations in all its many forms. As a consequence, such programs use a variety of approaches borrowed from disciplines as diverse as philosophy, ecology, and psychology. Some programs emphasize critical thinking and critical discourse, collaborative learning and multilingualism. Other programs focus on the use of the ecological model to enhance understanding of social structures and the diffusion of change, still other programs focus on the nature of inclusion and consensus and how best to translate those concepts into practice, not only at the classroom level but at the school and community level as well.

There is a danger in multicultural education programming of letting the political rhetoric and the academic research agenda overshadow the benefits of designing and implementing interesting and lively opportunities for children to learn. In fact, the reasons to use a multicultural approach in schools are simple and compelling.

— A multicultural approach makes learning more interesting and relevant to children's lives.

— A multicultural approach gives all students a forum in which to share information about who they are, how they live, what is important to them and their families.

— A multicultural approach gives students another lens through which to view history and society.

— A multicultural approach encourages tolerance and respect and supports notions of social reform and community cohesion.

Oral Histories

It is often the case that when a teacher says the word "history" to a group of youngsters there is a collective groan as eyes roll back and students brace for the worst. History can evoke images of dusty books, dimly lit libraries, and the tedious memorization of names and dates that take a long time to learn and a short time to forget. Fortunately, oral histories have none of those characteristics.

The broadest and simplest definition of an oral history is the reminiscences and recollections of living people concerning the past. These recollections can be passed down orally from generation to generation or may be the oral memories of an individual who was present at a specific time and event.

The only caveat is that the story is "collected" by an interviewer and then transcribed into text with some accompanying narrative or explanation that fleshes out the background of the storyteller and the particular situation. The topic is fairly irrelevant as long as it is about an actual memory or incident. Topics can be virtually anything from surviving a flood, putting food by, building a boat, memories of school days, tales of courage and moments of sheer hilarity and electrifying suspense.

The elements of a good oral history are the same as the elements of a good story. There are vibrant and fully realized characters such as; an eccentric aunt, Uncle so and so who was captured by pirates, the strongest man in the village or the lady across the street who loved cats. Each one of these people has a role in the tale and, most importantly, exists or existed in real life. There are problems to be solved. They can range from the grave to the mundane such as; harvesting food in a year with no rain, surviving the great depression, building a dyke against a flood or how to fix a roof, make a quilt or build a house without using nails.

The solutions to these problems or, in literary terms, the resolution, often illustrate everything from outstanding resourcefulness to blatant stupidity. The voice or the point of view of the oral history is that of the person telling the story.

The researcher acts as the invisible narrator who only adds those things, which help enhance or illuminate the dark corners of the tale that may be opaque to the reader. Finally the language or tone that the oral history takes is, and should be, true to the "teller". It is not the job of the oral historian to change the person's syntax and make them more or less educated, sophisticated or different from who they are. An oral history is not an exercise in creative writing but an exercise in telling the truth as someone else knows it.

Oral histories can be turned into books, articles, displays, and even videos. They are also a perfect venue for developing multicultural curriculum in schools. There is a compelling quote from the poet Rilke that ultimately summarizes what oral histories actually do.. *"Who ever tells the story shapes the world" The* oral history is the story, what a teacher does with it can shape the world.

The Steps in an Oral History Project

What follows is an abbreviated outline of the steps in an oral history project. For more complete information please see *Telling stories, writing lives: a guide to using oral history folklore and folklife.*

Getting started

The hardest part of an oral history is to decide on the topic. As students and teachers think about topics, perhaps the most salient question to answer is " will it make a good story". Think about events and people in a community that are pivotal. Wars, floods, and desperate times are natural starting points and usually come instantly to mind.

Another avenue to explore is memorable moments in people's lives such as weddings, births, chance meetings, and significant life choices. . These projects can result in stories of humor and grace that are informative as well as interesting. Families are full of these stories and they run the gamut from the serious to the romantic. How grandparents came to live where they do is a good start for an oral history on immigration.

How uncles and aunts learned their professions or met one another are opportunities for oral history around work and romance. How great aunt so and so learned to ride a horse or make a quilt or won a special prize at school are all part of the significant fabric of people's lives and are good choices for oral histories. The point to remember is that the stuff of life is the stuff of oral histories.

Where to go, who to interview and how

Once teachers and students have settled on a topic, the next hurdle in an oral history project is gathering information. This entails finding people to talk to, convincing them that that is a good idea, and finally, figuring out what to say. Gaining access is a term that refers to identifying and locating individuals that know about the topic. The interview is made up of a series of questions that encourages the speaker to tell his or her story. The most common mistakes that students make are to

a) pick topics that on the surface sound great but are in reality too difficult,

b) not find the right people to interview and

c) structure a weak interview.

The only real way to avoid making these mistakes is to practice. It is important to practice writing and doing interviews, as well as picking topics and designing projects that have a reasonable comfort level. For example, it would be unwise for students to decide to do an oral history project that requires them to travel great distances, or only interview very famous people. The likely-hood of failure would be high.

Interview guides are available and are helpful for the first time oral historian. When it comes to format and structure, there is no reason to reinvent the wheel. A good commercial interview guide can save students and teachers time and headaches as it provides useful suggestions and gives a solid structure from which to work.

The most accessible and fertile ground for oral history projects are in students' families and communities. Family and community oral history projects are very meaningful to students as they represent a celebration of easily recognizable individual and collective experience. Everyone loves to "know the hero" of the tale and local projects allow that to happen.

A gold mine of information exists in the elderly people in a community. What was life like fifty years ago is a wonderful place to start especially for school age children. Elderly people are usually interested in youngsters and generally enjoy their company. They are also often available for school visits and can become a real asset to any educational program but particularly one that is using oral history as part of a multicultural endeavor. Intergenerational perspectives are powerful and even more so when they include stories from diverse ethnic, racial and social groups.

Writing it up

Once students have collected stories and information the next step is to "write it up". The writing workshop is a perfect way to get lively and interesting pieces written. Important aspects of this process are talk and collaborative work. Students need time to assemble information and talk with one another about what they have and what they might do with it. Besides interviews, students can use photographs, souvenirs, news clippings and other artifacts relevant to the topic that they are researching. The most difficult part of the project comes when students must synthesize the information and "tell the story" in a voice that is true to the experience and to the person.

Finished products are only limited by the imagination and energy of the students. Oral history projects can be made into videos, displays, books for adults, books for children. They can be part of local celebrations as well as the focus for local and regional publications.

Oral History Projects

Oral history projects are about visibility. When students embark on a project those pieces of lived experience that have been in the shadows of families and communities come to light. What had once been invisible suddenly takes center stage. In a multicultural program this is particularly important as the experience of marginalized groups gets the same attention as the dominant group. Hero and heroines, problems and solutions emerge in the most unlikely places.

As a consequence, students and teachers have opportunities for discussions around such topics as courage, resourcefulness, fairness and opportunity but through the multicultural lens and anchored in the experience of students. This is a prime example of Simms Bishop's model of windows and mirrors. Oral histories can allow teachers and students to change the content of the curriculum as well as the way students gather information and understand each other.

Oral history projects reduce the distance between the student and the subject matter. It is one thing for students to learn about and discuss events and concepts from a theoretical perspective. It is a whole different matter to discuss the same events and concepts but anchored in the lived experiences of family and community members. From the perspective of Banks model, oral history projects offer teachers and students access to changing the structure of the curriculum by changing, in part, how some of the information is obtained and studied.

Oral history projects require a collaborative and inclusive working style. It is virtually impossible for students to carry out individual projects because there is too much involved; hence students need to work together. Furthermore oral history project are a bridge between the classroom and the community. It is essential that students go out into the community and it is equally essential the community come into the classroom. For students of minorities, this may be one of the first opportunities that their families can participate in a school-based activity as experts in a particular topic.

Oral history projects can illuminate social issues and problems and give students and teachers a forum for discussion, decision making and action. As students study their communities and listen to the stories of family members they see how those experiences highlight a need for action and social change. For example, an oral history project conducted in a small town in Connecticut focused on the plight of Portuguese fisherman, which ultimately resulted in new legislation in the fishing industry.

This is not to say that oral history projects can or should be the centerpiece of a multicultural program. However, these types of projects are a logical and interesting place to begin the discussion. They are not technically difficult to execute nor are they particularly expensive. They are worth doing if for no other reason than oral histories help us to see and to remember those pieces of the ordinary human experience that would be lost as it is in our stories that our lives have meaning.

Multicultural Publishing Projects

Publishing projects to support multicultural education projects can vary in a number of ways.

— *The authors* of multicultural publications can be the students in a classroom, selected students from a school, a group of young people recruited in the community for this purpose, teachers, or professional adult writers.

— *The audiences* can be the other students in a classroom, a whole school, students from different regions of the country (by means of exchanges), people in the immediate community, or even a national readership, if the works are published professionally.

— *The forms* the materials might take include a wall or hallway-mounted collage of texts, illustrations, and photographs. Or they might be a newsletter, a magazine, a handmade book, or a commercially printed book.

— *The genres and patterns* which organize the publications can take on interesting variety, also.

Patterns and Genres of Multicultural Publications

Readers expect patterns in the texts they read; but inexperienced writers often have difficulty finding a design and sticking to it. What are some useful patterns for works written for children?

The first set of patterns introduced below might be used by children who are writing their own books, or by adults writing for children. These ideas were collected by Sylvia Vardell.

— *Alphabet books.* (Animals, names, or objects presented from A to Z).

— *Counting books.* (Numbers from 0 to 10, 1 to 20; sets of 5 or 10; addition problems; telling time; counting money).

— *Predictable pattern books.* (This is... AI wish.. I like... Someday...)

— *Rhymes, songs, and poems.* (Anthologies, or one book containing a single poem)

— *Riddles, proverbs, jokes* (old favorites, ones collected in the community, new creations)

— *Retellings of traditional tales or religious stories* (including stories that were collected from sources in the community)

— *Personal narratives.* (First person accounts of individual experiences; or first person accounts told to the writer by a community person)

— *Vocabulary to learn or rules to demonstrate.* (A personal dictionary or guidebook for carrying out a procedure)

— *Biography or history.* (Based on interviews or research)

— *Autobiography of journals.* (Me, my family, my feelings)

— *Nonfiction or informational books* (about a favorite topic)

— *Concept books.* (Simple concept with examples given: colors, animals, senses).
— *How to do books.* (Clear instructions on how to build or create or do something).
— *Cookbooks.* (Anthologies or individual creations).
— *Word less picture books.* (In which a story is told entirely through pictures.
— *Favorite book formula.* (Imitate or innovate on the pattern of a favorite book).
— *Favorite character book.* (Make up a new adventure of a favorite character).
— *Original imaginative stories.* (Fictional characters or fantasy characters).
— *Art books.* (Single or mixed media collections of artwork with titles, captions, or stories).
— *Class anthologies.* (A mixture of all literary types).
— *Movable/pop-up books.* (Three dimension; moveable parts)
— *Shape books.* (Books in the physical shape of the topic, like letters, numbers, or shoes).
— *Bilingual books.* (Romanian/Romani, etc.)
— *Words/sounds.* (Featuring idioms, expressions, or initial consonants or vowel sounds, or syllables)

Longer Narrative Patterns

For more extended texts, narrative patterns are often used. There are a range of patterns around which narratives can be arranged some of them quite obvious, but a few of them less so.

1. *Sequential patterns.* The trappings of a traditional wedding could be highlighted as follows: At the start of the wedding feast, I ate a plum tart. But the bride still had not danced. By two o'clock I had eaten a plum tart and two hot crossed buns. But the bride still had not danced. By half past three I had eaten a plum tart, two hot crossed buns, and _______and so on.
2. *Amazing Grace.* In Carolyn Bench's book, Amazing Grace, a young girl growing up in a modern city is having a crisis of confidence over the school play. Her aunt from her native island inspires her with the confidence of her roots, and the girl eventually triumphs. Children in other cultures could use a similar message.
3. *The tension between traditional culture and modern culture.* In Sharon Bell Mathis' The 100 Penny Box, a hundred year-old grandmother keeps a penny from every year of her life and tells a story to go with each one to her young great-grandson, with whom she lives in a cramped urban apartment. The boy's mother has no use for the old woman's tales; and the boy is caught in between. This pattern bears recycling
4. *Plots that stem from characters and their problems.* Good stories can be developed by thinking of a character in her setting, wishing what a person would typically wish for in that place. The story is further developed as opposing forces or characters are brought into play.

Standards of Writing for Young People

As the patterns of writing grow more complex, writers must work hard to handle them well. Many professional writers say that good writing is revising. Many published authors seek out the company of writers' groups so they may share their works and receive suggestions. At many such workshops we have conducted, the suggestions writers offer each other tend to boil down to a fairly small set of recommendations. Suggestions such as the following are useful when writing fiction for children and young people:

— *Write within a genre*: If the story is realistic, don't have trees talking!

— Make it sound natural, but *write in patterns.*

— Create a *beginning* (in which characters are introduced and a problem is posed), a *middle* (in which the story is developed, and attempts are made to solve the problem), and an *end* (in which the problem is resolved and the characters' new circumstances are presented).

— Put the *Main Dramatic Question* close to the beginning.

— *Use words the way poets do*: for sound, meaning, and suggestion.

— *Put the child in the driver's* seat: That is, give the child a leading role in solving the problem.

— *Tell the truth:* don't offer unrealistic solutions to real problems.

— *Have the work be about something, but don't preach.* The most satisfying works seem on reflection to make some point. However, stories can teach by themselves without heavy-handed moralizing by the writer.

— *Show, don't tell* (Make the reader see, hear, smell, feel).

— *Trust the reader*. Don't explain everything.

— *Surprise your readers.*

— However realistic or even grim the characters' circumstances may be, *leave a ray of hope in your works.*

Writers' Workshops

There is a widely held belief that only certain gifted individuals can write anything worthwhile. Those who are not inherently gifted only embarrass themselves by attempting to write. Yet when one gazes on the portraits of those gifted individuals, hanging high on the walls of school classrooms, one perceives a curious pattern: They are all well dressed! They are all men! They are all white! (And they are almost all dead!). Perhaps it is not talent for writing that is in limited supply, but the expectation that many people, even young people, might have interesting things to say, in print.

Indeed, the multicultural writers' workshop movement has found and nurtured many fine writers who would not otherwise have been published. One of the most pleasing realizations that followed this effort in the United States was that these writers really had quite a lot to say: and, once published, they have stayed in print through their own popularity.

Even in schools, writers' workshop movements have encouraged personal authorship among students, and have had very positive results: (1) They nurture the students' self-expression and develop their self-esteem, and (2) they open other students' eyes to the experiences and ideas of their classmates from every neighborhood and from every ethnicity. (The mirror and window phenomenon again). Teachers also like the fact that personal authorship leads students to identify more closely with professional authors, and look more seriously at the author's craft.

Without denying that some people have more gifts for writing than others, we can say confidently that virtually any student can be helped to unleash what he or she wants to say on paper. What is needed are *permission to write about things that matter to the writer, real audiences who will receive the writing for what it says, frequent opportunities to write,* and *models and demonstrations of the process of writing.* The process of writing referred to in the last sentence has come to be understood to be something like the following:

The Writing Process

Is there one process that all writers go through to produce a finished piece? Surely not. But there is one description of the writing process that seems to come the closest to what most writers do when they compose. This is the writing process model put forward by Donald Murray and Donald Graves. This model has proved useful for organizing writing instruction, too.

The writing process provides a means by which a student begins with an idea, and gradually shapes that idea on the page to the point that it successfully communicates to the readers, and builds connections between the readers and the writer around the theme developed by the author out of the original idea. It is a step-by-step process through which students become credible authors, and writing becomes a vehicle for clarifying and expressing ideas.

According to the model of the writing process we will use here, most thoughtful pieces of writing go through three steps: rehearsing, drafting, and revising. Those that are to be published go through two more: editing and publishing. Does every piece of writing go through these steps, in this order? Again, of course not. It's very likely that young people will move back and forth through these steps, though they will most commonly use that order. In the pages that follow, we will explain each of these steps, and pause to show activities that help young people learn at each one. Again, it should be said that the writing process described here may be used in all subject areas, although special applications to the disciplines will be shared later in this guide.

Rehearsing. Rehearsing is the act of gathering information and collecting our thoughts. We survey the ideas we have available to us on a topic, and begin to plan a way into writing about it.

Drafting. Drafting is the act of setting ideas out on paper. Drafting is tentative, experimental. We write down our ideas so we can see what we have to say about out topic. Once they are there, we can make them clearer, even elegant.

When we are drafting, it is no time to be critical with our ideas, their form, or their spelling and handwriting: the time for all that will come later.

Most young writers (indeed, most writers) don't have the habit of writing more than one version of a paper. Proficient writers do. "Writing is rewriting," they say. We'll need to encourage students to think of writing as drafting.

Revising. After our paper is written in draft form, we can start to make it better. We'll improve the paper in two careful stages. At the revising stage, we want to see what we had to say, and decide how it can be said better. We are concerned that our ideas be clear, and that they be presented in the right form. We are still not worrying about spelling, handwriting, or grammatical correctness at this stage, although of course they are important: These issues will be dealt with in the next stage: the proof-reading or editing stage.

Editing. Once a paper has been drafted and revised, it is ready for editing. Editing is the final polishing a undergoes before it goes public. Editing is held off for last, because paragraphs or even pages may have been cut or added in the revising stage. After the piece is in final form, but before it is widely shared, is the time for editing.

The habit of editing must be taught. The habit consists of three things:

— caring that the paper be correct;

— being aware of errors;

— knowing how to set them straight.

Publishing: Publishing is the final stage of the writing process, and in important ways publishing drives the whole enterprise. The prospect of sharing what they have to say with an audience makes many students want to write, and rewrite, and smooth out and refine—especially if they've seen other students' work received with appreciation and delight. Publishing also lets students see what each other is doing. A good idea is contagious; and anything from an interesting topic, to a plot structure, to a way to use dialogue, to the habit of taking risks with spelling may be shared through the process of publishing.

A Demonstration Writing Workshop

Tied to the above description of the writing process, of what effective writers do in order to produce a viable work, is a strategy for teaching the process: The *writing workshop*. Writing workshops can be done in classroom, even primary grade classrooms; or they may be offered for adult groups. Perhaps the best way to visualize what a writing workshop looks like is to consider this Ascript@ for a very first writing workshop, as it is introduced in the Reading & Writing for Critical Thinking Project. The instructions are written for the person directing the workshop.

PREPARE FIVE TOPICS. You will need to have prepared in advance four or five topics about subjects that are lively and important to you just now. Take care that these are topics from "the human carnival," describing events and feelings that you are likely to have in common with the people in your workshop.

DISPLAY THE TOPICS. Begin by writing those topics on a sheet of newsprint, or overhead transparency. Explain that you (and they) will be writing short papers in this session about things that matter to you. You have thought of these topics as possibilities, and would like their help in choosing one of them to write about.

OTHERS INTERVIEW YOU. Request that they interview you about each topic, asking questions such as, "What interests you most about this topic?' "Tell us more about _______." "Why did you choose this topic?" Answer their questions, and as you do, make it clear why one particular topic stands out to you from the others—perhaps for its freshness, vividness, or poignancy; perhaps for its manageable scope. (Take time to point out that topics that are too abstract, too ambitious, or that you don't have enough information about are better left for another day).

OTHERS LIST TOPICS. Now ask them to do the same: make a list of four or five possible topics that matter to them, that they might like to write a short piece about.

OTHERS INTERVIEW EACH OTHER ABOUT THEIR TOPICS. After everyone has had four or five minutes to make a list, ask people to pair up and share their lists. Partners should then interview each other about their topics, just as they interviewed you, so that each person can be helped to identify the one topic that seems most interesting to other people, and to herself.

MAKE A CLUSTER. Now make a cluster of details about your topic. Write your topic in a circle in the center of the page, then write subtopics as "satellites" around your main topic, and add subtopics to each of those.

OTHERS INTERVIEW YOU ABOUT YOUR CLUSTER. Invite the participants to ask you about the details you listed, and the ways they go together. In short, have them help you "find your story." Mark prominently on your cluster the part you will write about.

OTHERS MAKE CLUSTERS AND INTERVIEW EACH OTHER. Now invite the participants to think through the topics they chose in the previous step, and make a cluster for the ideas they associate with it. After they have had seven or eight minutes to do so, ask them to stop and interview each other about their clusters, in order to "find their stories." They may have listed more details than they can work into a short paper; so after discussing the details with a partner, they should now mark the most interesting and relevant parts of their clusters.

EVERYONE WRITE FOR AN INTERVAL. Explain that you will all be writing drafts that can be changed before they are shared. The important thing is for people to get their ideas out on paper. They should write without stopping or going back for the allotted period of time (allow about 20 minutes for this). Be sure to tell them to write on every other line. You write, too, either on an overhead or on chart paper.

SHOW A PAPER THAT COMMUNICATES, BUT THAT CAN BE IMPROVED IN SOME RESPECT. You may need to prepare this ahead of time, but you should have a paper that conveys real ideas, but that also has something about it that could use revision— such as flat, colorless language that "tells" rather than "shows." Display the paper (either on newsprint or on an overhead) and ask the participants to say first what they find pleasing about it, and then to help you make it communicate better. Presumably they will call attention to the flat language, and you can then ask volunteers for suggestions for more vivid wording for each dull spot.

Take a moment now to talk about the difference between positive, constructive comments that help us make our writing better, and negative comments that discourage us. Positive comments include naming specific parts we liked—those that are most aptly described, most vivid, most surprising, most enjoyable—and saying what we liked about them. They also include asking about parts that are confusing to us or ambiguous, or where we would like more information.

Also, make a point about ownership: the idea that the ultimate responsibility for the paper rests with the writer. Others can tell us their reactions, and those are valuable to writers, but the decision of whether to change something change it always rests with the writer.

OTHERS READ PAPERS TO PARTNERS, FOR COMMENTS AND CRITIQUES. They should now take turns sharing their papers, and first comment on the meaning of the paper, and name what they liked about the paper. Later they can see if there are parts that could be made clearer or more vivid—just as they helped you do with your own. Writers should put in any additions or clarifications on their papers in the lines they left for that purpose.

WRITE REFINED DRAFTS OF YOUR PAPERS. Now everyone writes again for fifteen minutes or so, creating a new draft that improves on the previous one—we hope with the benefits of the conferring that just occurred.

READ TO THE WALL. Before the participants take the last step of sharing their papers with the larger group, ask each person to read his or her paper aloud to the wall, and listen for words that can be changed, unclear parts that can be improved, and unnecessary words or phases that can be omitted.

ASK VOLUNTEERS TO READ FROM THE "AUTHOR'S CHAIR." Designate a chair at "center stage" in the room, from which a volunteer will read his or her paper to the whole group. Remind the others ahead of time that after the reading, they will be asked to find one thing that they liked about the paper, and also ask the writer one question. Share four or five papers with the whole group in this way.

IN RETROSPECT, NOTE THESE GENERAL POINTS:

— The teacher served as a model, treating writing as a "studio craft," analogous to the ways he or she might teach a class in pottery making, or painting.

— The topics came from everyone's own interests and experiences, rather than from assignments.

— The thrust of the whole exercise was to communicate to a real audience something that interested the writer

— Peers helped each other communicate their messages more elegantly, instead of teachers receiving the papers for purposes of grading.

THE ESSENTIAL NEEDS OF A WRITING CLASSROOM: TIME, OWNERSHIP, AND DEMONSTRATION.

— *Time*: Writing workshops should be scheduled at regular intervals so that students know when they will have opportunities to write, get help with, and share their ideas.

— *Ownership*: Students should have opportunities to choose their own topics, or at least their own approach to topics. When conferences are conducted to help students improve writing, their "ownership" of the work must still be respected, with freedom left for them to choose which advice to follow.

— *Demonstration*: Teaching writing, as we said, is a "studio craft," with attention to the process of creating well written works. The teacher should demonstrate every phase of the process so students will know how effective writing is done.

The Dynamics of Illustrating Books for Children.

When we have conducted workshops with the intention of producing professionally published materials, we have often given an orientation to potential illustrators of the books, too. Picture books create unique challenges and opportunities to illustrators, since they sustain the same narrative over 16, 32, or 64 pages, and require many illustrations that reflect both the continuity of the text and the changing dramatic contours. The following are some points we often make with illustrators.

— *Characterization* (How does the illustrator makes us know each character by appearance? How are parts of a character used to denote him or her?)

— *Perspective and positioning* (Where is the central character positioned? From what perspective do we view the action? In what direction are things moving? It is said that a character seen on the left hand side of the page may appear to be more in control of things than a character seen on the right. The same is true of a character seen higher on the page, and larger).

— *Lay-out* (Double-page spreads can suggest expansiveness or serenity; whereas single page spreads move the story along more quickly. If the character is seen in several pictures on the same page, this often suggests that things are moving too quickly for him, and he might soon lose control).

— *Borders* (Borders contain the action. When actions spread out across the borders, it appears too large or powerful to contain).

— *Page turns* (There is a drama of the turning page, which creates suspense on the right- hand page before the turn, and resolves it on the left hand page after the turn).

— *The last page* (The last page often serves as a visual commentary, denouement, or punch line.)

— *The interaction of picture and text* (Good artists create a complementarity: What is stated in the text need not be illustrated, and vice versa).

5

Challenges of International Education

The impact of intensified globalization is possibly the most often cited challenge facing the field of comparative and international education at this point in time. Somewhat paradoxically, interest in globalization has attracted many new scholars and professionals to comparative and international research-but, at the same time, it has generated critiques of traditionally accepted modes of operation and frameworks of analysis.

At the heart of this are challenges to the prominence of the nation-state as the primary unit of analysis in so much work carried out within the field. Global forces, it is argued, are dramatically changing the role of the state in education, and demanding increased attention to be paid to factors operating beyond the national level.

The mechanisms and processes driving globalization are thus prioritized for examination, as is the increased significance of multi-lateral agencies in shaping global policy debates and agendas. However, recognition of the fact that the effects of globalization differ from place to place, draws attention back to the nature and implications of such differential effects-even at the national level.

Few empirically grounded studies have compared these differences in any sustained way to date- and those that have been carried out have largely focused upon Western industrial societies or the newly industrialized economies of East Asia.

The impact of globalization on the poorer, post-colonial societies of the "South" has received much less attention, despite the dramatic implications for development processes in such contexts. Here there is much urgent work for the field of comparative and international education in the future.

The challenges posed by globalization, however, also pull in other directions reflecting what Arnove and Torres have usefully characterized as the "dialectic of the global and the local". To cite Giddens, globalization is a complex set of processes, not a single one. And these operate in a contradictory or oppositional fashion. Most people think of it as simply 'pulling away' power or influence from local communities and nations into the global arena. And indeed this is one of its consequences. Nations do lose some of the economic power they once had. However, it is also has an opposite effect. Globalization not only pulls upwards, it pushes downwards, creating new pressures for local autonomy.

This draws attention to the fact that national and local cultures can and do play a significant role in mediating global influences. From this perspective, units of analysis that pay attention to the local effects of globalization are also prioritized. This, in turn, adds renewed legitimacy to qualitative modes of research that emphasize grassroots fieldwork, ethnography and the interpretive/hermeneutic paradigms that emphasize micro-level studies of education in context. While much more can be said about the challenges posed by globalization, it is argued that, despite its pervasive influence, numerous other challenges also face the field, and demand attention in their own right.

Related to the latter methodological issues, for example, are very significant paradigmatic and epistemological implications raised by increased sensitivity to culture and context. This is reflected in the impact on the field of post-structural scholarship, and of the application and critique of post-modernist and post-colonial theoretical frameworks.

In many respects post-colonial frameworks also draw attention to the challenges generated by dramatically changed geopolitical realities; from the decline of colonialism; from attention to culture and identity; and from the turbulent latter years of the 20th century.

This is reflected in the field's heightened awareness of the dangers of ethnocentrism, and its recognition of the problematic use of distinctions and terminology relating to, for example, "developed" and "developing" countries, and the "North" and the "South".

For the present writer, the methodological challenges of such developments point most strongly to the need for new forms of international relationships in terms of comparative and international research; to the importance of collaborative research and partnerships between "insiders" and "outsiders"; to research and development work that is more sensitive to local, social constructions of reality; and to strategies that facilitate the strengthening of research capacity within the South.

In many respects, the rational for this is related to efforts to help "bridge" the gap between educational research and its potential to improve policy and practice. This is, in itself, one of the most prominent challenges faced by educational research communities world-wide.

The widening constituency of policy-makers and practitioners who have taken renewed interest in comparative and international research are certainly looking for findings that will be of use to them in their professional activities. While this is a complex arena in which there are few simple answers, the challenges raised by such diversity of audiences are of considerable and renewed significance for the field. Relatedly, the intensification of international competition, spurred on by globalization, neo-liberalism and marketization, has major implications for cross-national studies of educational achievement.

If the funding of research is increasingly linked to commercial interests, for example, the potential for critical theory, or for alternative cultural perspectives to influence the construction of new knowledge, may be increasingly challenged-even in, paradoxically, the new "knowledge" economy. So questions of power and "whose knowledge counts?" in the process of development arise, perhaps, more strongly than ever before.

To this we could add the challenges raised by rapid advances in information and communications technology (ICT). As many have pointed out, these are many and varied-but it is argued that their implications arise most strongly in cross-cultural contexts, where the "digital divide" is greatest, and both their potential benefits and problems deserve urgent attention.

Growing tensions between the global, the national and the local, thus, so fundamentally underpin all aspects of contemporary society and development, that a similarly fundamental reconceptualization of the field of comparative and international education is required, if we are to more effectively address such issues.

The international on-line debate stimulated by the present publication, will also, helpfully, keep dialogue very much alive and make an ongoing contribution. Returning to the issues raised in the two special numbers of Comparative Education, and to the writer's earlier work, the following themes emerge most strongly. Firstly, it is argued that it is the comparative and international research focus that is at the forefront of the resurgence of interest in the field - and it is to ways of reconceptualizing research that we must increasingly look in the future. This includes theoretical, methodological, substantive and organizational dimensions. Work such as that by Bray and Thomas on multi-levels of analysis helps to point one way forward by acknowledging the potential of many different units of analysis. Other pointers may come from pioneering efforts to promote more genuinely collaborative international teams-especially linking different "territories" such as the North and the South, or policy and practice. Such organizational possibilities then have major implications for the theoretical and methodological frameworks that we might employ.

Sensitive to the differences between various theoretical discourses, Cowen, however, wisely cautions against a search for the one "right" mode- and celebrates the diversity of comparative educations. Writing within the second "response" special number of Comparative Education, Kazamias makes an impassioned plea for closer linkages between the humanities and the social sciences within the multi-disciplinary field. For Kazamias, the reclamation of the historical dimension of the field would counterbalance its post-World War II dehumanization, and represent a priority direction for the future. Whatever position we might adopt with regard to the role of history, there is certainly much to be gained from a more effective bridging with the best of past scholarship within the field, even as we look towards the future.

6

Strategies of Multicultural Education

School librarians are faced with the challenge of linking students from widely varying backgrounds to information sources and drawing them into patterns of regular library use. By creating a positive climate, the school library can provide English as a second language (ESL) students with a place for learning, sharing, and personal growth.

The ESL students were introduced to the library at a time when no other classes were there. Each student was given a diagram of the library, then walked through each area beginning at the entrance. Hands-on activities were provided, such as practice in using the copy machine.

Thereafter, students returned to the library on an individual basis, or in pairs, with a specific request to the librarian; at this time, individual explanations and demonstrations were given of the various areas and their uses.

Eventually, students were sent to the librarian with individual assignments. By this time, students were familiar with the library staff and did not hesitate to approach them for help. Students were encouraged to use the library before school, after school, and during study hall periods. As a result, the ESL students found the library to be a safe and welcoming place and became frequent users.

To draw ESL students into a pattern of regular library use, the library established a collection of reading materials in their first languages. To meet the full range of interests and reading abilities, collections of fiction and non-fiction books in Spanish, Arabic, and Portuguese were borrowed for extended periods through Interlibrary Loan. With school library funds, a small collection of Portuguese books, a weekly Portuguese newspaper, a Spanish newspaper, and foreign language dictionaries were purchased. Spanish magazines were contributed by the Spanish language teacher.

High-interest, low-reading-level paperbacks in English were borrowed from a local public library's literacy collection. At the request of the ESL teacher, these books were housed in the ESL classroom for easy access during classroom times. A listening station with a cassette player and headphone and a collection of read-along books in English were made available in the library conference room. Most books were classics that are required reading for high school students. In addition, a collection of wordless books was borrowed from several public libraries.

Many elementary school ESL teachers report multiple uses of these books, including promotion of oral language and conversation skills, development of sequence and prediction skills, and development of vocabulary skills.

For all students, but especially for ESL students, the optimal learning process involves connecting new ideas with old knowledge. To provide materials required for this, the librarian introduced the use of advanced organizers, an essential instructional strategy proposed by Ausubel to enhance classroom learning. That the information-processing system of humans is a set of ideas that provides anchors for new information or ideas, that in turn provides a storehouse when new meanings are acquired.

Central to enhancing the learning process for students with language needs is the technique of building learning upon prior learning and knowledge. Based on this view of how learners process information, and the realization that much of the material to be learned by ESL students is completely new and unrelated to anything they know, the librarian created opportunities for ESL students to gain essential prior knowledge through the use of advance organizers.

Collaboration between the librarian and the ESL teacher resulted in a list of key themes and subject areas related to the ESL text and curriculum. Appropriate materials were acquired, borrowed, and collected by the librarian for use in both the media center and in the ESL classroom. Because this strategy relies heavily on visuals and pictorial materials, a picture file was developed for advance organizers. To collect materials suitable for use as advance organizers, the librarian used references for collecting visuals with pictures of all kinds, especially designed for second language learners, a directory of resource organizations, and various bibliographies.

The school library organized a program with speakers on occupations, career choices, and vocational and education options for the ESL students through the local community college. Representing the college were an admissions officer, a Spanish-speaking counselor from Access to Opportunity (a counseling and mentor program for ESL, at-risk, low-income, and disadvantaged students), and a Spanish-speaking counselor from the Education Opportunity Center (a pre-admission center for ESL students needing counseling in language competency, financial aid, admission requirements, GED information, etc.).

The program was held in Spanish and English in the school library with an interpreter for the Portuguese students. Follow-up appointments were made and the counselor from the Educational Opportunity Center returned weekly to the school library for individual counseling.

The school library has a unique role in the integration of cultural differences within the school community. Because library services are essential to all segments of the school population and school activities, the librarian holds a strategic position as an integrator, coordinator, negotiator, unifier, and equalizer.

While a class of English-speaking students was researching Christmas customs around the world, the ESL class was researching Christmas traditions in the United States. The librarian offered to co-ordinate an intercultural program between the two classes to exchange Christmas customs and traditions. When the ESL students were researching the history and foods of Thanksgiving, the librarian proposed the preparation of a Thanksgiving dinner. Ultimately, the ESL teacher had a

Thanksgiving dinner brought into her class for her students.

One literacy activity took shape when the school librarian observed that senior students were assigned to the high school library for Spanish IV Independent Study. It seemed that there were opportunities for these students to improve their Spanish literacy if Spanish-speaking students could be in the library at the same time. This would help the Spanish-speaking students improve their English literacy skills and would help to promote multicultural understanding.

By consulting with the ESL teacher, Spanish-speaking ESL students were identified and an examination of their schedules showed that some of them could be scheduled into the library for the same period as the Spanish IV students. Alliances were formed with the Spanish and ESL teachers, and two student literacy groups were formed. Students were informed by the teachers of the purpose of the groups, and that they would be graded by the librarian for effort and participation. Spanish/English dictionaries were available at each meeting.

Initial sessions were centered around oral communication in Spanish and English. Because the students were strangers to each other, the flow of conversation of these early sessions was directed by the librarian.

In the beginning, there were periods of silence. However, as the meetings progressed, barriers were overcome and the project took on a life of its own. Conversation became natural and comfortable. Students began requesting a non-directed format of conversation.

Spanish was spoken during half of the period, and English was spoken during the other half. At times, conversations and discussions would alternate between Spanish-speaking students speaking in English, while English-speaking students responded in Spanish. At other times, the order would be reversed.

Culture-specific dialogues were created. For example, when teenage culture in Mexico and the United States was explored, recognition of similarities and differences clarified false assumptions and generalizations. As English-speaking students sought knowledge and information about the social, cultural, economic, and political issues of Mexico, the Spanish-speaking students became information givers, thus gaining a new status.

Following the oral communicative stage, the group moved on to reading in both Spanish and English. Following the reading of each article, students translated the article in their own words, then each student provided an individual interpretation of the article in English and Spanish.

The writing segment of this literacy activity began with students agreeing to be ethnographers by observing what was happening in and outside of class, at school functions, and in interactions between ESL students and native-English-speaking students. Students agreed to keep a journal to record their observations of differences and to reflect on whether these differences were cultural. This served as a springboard to multicultural understanding.

Finally, journal writing was introduced between students in both languages. Through journal writing, a sense of developing friendships was observed.

Noticeable, also, was the interaction of these students as they met between classes and in the hallways.

Although initiated as a literacy activity, these group meetings also produced a greater appreciation and understanding of cultural diversity, empowered students, and provided an opportunity for friendships to form. The English-speaking students began to acknowledge the expertise of the Spanish-speaking students and sought help from them more often than from the dictionary. In turn, the Spanish-speaking students developed new friends and were empowered by their new helping role.

In short, the development of skills in using the library and its resources is an essential part of learning English. Non-native English speakers may have an even greater need for library skills than native speakers. Although they may not have achieved the English proficiency necessary for expressing their learning needs, they may need information that native speakers take for granted. ESL students must be given the tools that will enable them to succeed in the American education system.

7

Strategies of Learning Development

The 1992, the National Education Commission reconfirmed the commitment of His Majesty's Government to achieve universal primary education and to improve the quality of education in line with the Jomtien Declaration of Education for All (1990) and the summit goals of the United Nations Convention on the Rights of the Child (1990). The 1992 Commission endorsed most of the policy and programmatic recommendations contained in the Basic and Primary Education Master Plan. The new democratic government gave top priority to primary and basic education as a means of promoting basic human rights and as a strategy for poverty alleviation. Among other priorities, the 1992 Commission emphasised the urgent need to address the educational needs of different linguistic groups and ethnic minorities, and to bring about the long overdue quality improvement of the education system.

The Basic and Primary Education Project (BPEP) was designed to identify efficient management structures, to expand and enhance access and learning conditions, and to improve the quality of primary and basic education. BPEP was implemented in a phased manner, covering 19 districts in the year 1992/93, adding six districts in 1993/94, and extending to another 15 districts in 1994/95 (thus totalling 40 of the 75 districts in the country). It was executed with the financial assistance of DANIDA (US$ 16.28 million), UNICEF (US$ 4.64 million), JICA (US$ 15.73 million) and IDA (loan of US$ 30.60 million). The external assistance amounted to 26% of the total BPEP expenditure and the remaining 74% (NRs. 10,976 million) was borne by His Majesty's Government.

BPEP adopted a management structure which led to the efficient delivery of project inputs on one hand, and which facilitated the development of programmes and materials on the other.

BPEP has made a significant contribution in programme development of different components, including:

- development of the new primary education curriculum;
- revision of textbooks, teachers guides and development of supplementary materials;
- development of schools and Resource Centres;
- development of teachers training packages;
- development of management training programmes;
- development of non-formal education packages;
- development of the special education programme; and
- development of the women's education programme

BPEP implemented several activities in order to improve the quality of primary education in the project districts. A summary of the activities is presented in Table 1.

Table 1.

Achievement Status of BPEP Activities in Quality Improvement

Quality Improvement	*Achievement*
Implementation of primary education curriculum (Grades 1 to 5)	Nation-wide
Distribution of textbooks and teachers guides (Grades 1 to 5)	Nation-wide
Distribution of supplementary materials (districts)	40
Teacher training (teachers)	
— 2.5 months	8,511
— Grade Teaching	994
— Multi-Grade Teaching	3,943
— Extra-curricular	1,448
— Whole School Approach	37,690
— Resource Centre (RC)	
— Resource Centres	669
— Resource Persons on duty	569
— Basic RP management training	834
— Advanced RP management training	482

BPEP adopted a strategy mix of constructing additional classrooms, promoting non-formal programmes, and gradual introduction of compulsory primary education. The achievements made toward promoting equitable access to the basic and primary education are summarised in Table 2.

Table 2.

Promoting Equitable Access: Achievement for 1992-1998.

Improvement Physical Facilities	*Achievement*
New classroom construction	14,112
Classroom rehabilitation	7,522
Furniture for classrooms	11,646
RC building construction and furnishing	306
DEO buildings	19
Distribution of manuals for school building maintenance (sets)	7,690
Maintenance training	7,152
Maintenance tools (sets)	7.152
Non-Formal Education Programme	
Out-of-School Programme I	114.197
Out-of-School Programme II	336,156
Out-of-School Programme III	1,500
Women's Education Programme I	204,397
Women's Education Programme II	56,416
Women's Education Programme III	11,049
Adult Education Programme I	39,505
Adult Education Programme II	6,154
New Literacy Programme I	265
Chelibeti Programme	19,818
Women Education Programme	
Recruitment of female teachers	4,151
Training for female teachers	3,588
Special Education Programme	
District Disability Survey	15
Scholarships for disabled children	2,700
Early Childhood Development (ECD)	
Training of ECD teachers	2,232
Establishment of ECD classes	1,200
Compulsory Primary Education (CPE)	
CPE initiated in districts	5

BPEP also institutionalised several measures to strengthen the management of basic and primary education at different levels. On the basis of the positive experiences from BPEP implementation, HMG has made the following policy decisions:

— Adoption of the Resource Centre structure and provision of School Management Committees as a tier of educational management

— Government decision to provide at least 10 days of recurrent training to every teacher each year

— Placement of at least one female teacher in each primary school

— Inclusion of ECD component in the regular structure of the MOE

— Decision to introduce the coupon system instead of the reimbursement policy for receiving free textbooks from dealers in the districts

— Inclusion of parents and representatives from disadvantaged communities on School Management Committees

— Gradual introduction of Compulsory Primary Education (CPE) in all 75 districts

The Primary Education Development Project

The Primary Education Development Project (PEDP) was implemented in 1993 as a complement to BPEP with focus on the development and consolidation of the teacher training system. PEDP was financed with an ADB loan of US$ 20 million. The most significant contribution of PEDP was establishment of a network of nine primary teacher-training centres. Specific details of PEDP's contribution toward improving the quality of the basic and primary education are outlined below.

— The National Centre for Educational Development has been established as an apex body of primary teacher training with the responsibility of planning, programming and managing primary teacher training, as well as training school supervisors, Headmasters and education management personnel. The infrastructure of NCED has been built in Sanothimi, Bhaktapur.

— Nine Primary Teacher Training Centres have been established in Bhojpur, Sunsari, Janakpur, Kavre, Bara, Tanahun, Rupandehi, Surkhet and Doti Districts to provide long-term training for untrained primary school teachers and school management training for the primary school Headmasters of 75 districts.

— Six District Education Office buildings have been completed.

— The project has succeeded in providing training for 22,141 teachers, 4,659 Headmasters, 264 supervisors and 115 education management personnel.

— 1,495 schools have been built and 1,425 schools have been provided with furniture out of 1,500 targeted schools. Toilets and drinking water have been provided to 950 out of 1,000 targeted schools.

— The project has supported the improvement of physical facilities (rehabilitation and educational materials) of the Faculties of Education of Birgunj

Campus and Sanothimi Campus and provided fund for producing qualified manpower for primary education (B.Ed. in primary education).

Promising strategies

The 1990s have remained a decade of development and consolidation efforts in the primary and basic education area of Nepal. Experiences gained and lessons learned from these efforts point to some promising strategies that could make a difference in optimising the quality and efficiency of the primary and basic education system. Some of the promising strategies are:

— co-operative and participatory planning processes at the central, district and community levels;

— establishment of Resource Centres and provision of Resource Persons (each for about 15-25 schools) to create a training, supervision and support system for the qualitative improvement of the primary and basic education;

— integration of special education programmes with primary and basic education;

— encouragement and recognition of local quality improvement efforts such as development of the RC as a community resource, and development and use of teaching/learning materials at the school level;

— management and use of educational information at the school and RC levels; and

— nutrition (afternoon food) programme for children in the rural areas as motivation to enrol and complete primary education.

A number of high-level government documents guide the development of curricula. They include the Secondary Education Perspective Plan (1996-2011), the Secondary Education Action Plan (1997-2002) and a recent High-Level Education Commission Report (1998).

Organisational Structure and Mechanisms in Curriculum Reform

The curriculum planned at the central level is modified by all the processes leading to its adoption. In the classroom at the secondary level most institutionalized activity is centrally controlled.

Ministry of education

The task of initiating educational activities throughout Nepal lies with the Ministry of Education (MOE). The Ministry is responsible for educational planning and management, as well as in improving service delivery systems across the country. MOE is composed of three divisions: Planning; General Administration; and Educational Administration.

Educational programmes and services are prepared by: the Curriculum Development Centre;

— the Secondary Education Development Centre; the Distance Education Centre;

— the Office of the Controller of Examinations;

— the National Centre for Educational Development;

— the regional education directorates and district education offices.

From July 1999 a new structure will be implemented with the formation of a Department of Secondary, Education, containing a Primary and Basic Education Division and a Secondary and Higher Secondary Division. This will separate policy making from executive actions.

A high-level National Curriculum Council (NCC), chaired by the Minister of Education, approves all curricula and guides the detailed developmental work of the Curriculum Development Centre (CDC) by setting operational and administrative policy.

The NCC forms ad-hoc technical committees when additional advice is required. Matters concerning the relevance of curricula drafted by CDC may be referred to such a technical committee if the NCC feels additional advice is necessary.

The CDC is responsible for the maintenance, transmission and renewal of the school-level curriculum and is also concerned with pre-primary education. (See below for further discussion of CDC).

The Secondary Leaving Certificate Board sets policies and makes decisions relating to the School-Leaving Certificate (SLC), which are then implemented by the Office of the Controller of Examinations (OCE).

A reformed SLC, with single subject certification is planned for July 2001. The courses leading to this examination are to be implemented from grade 9, beginning in July 1999.

The Secondary Education Development Centre

The Secondary Education Development Centre (SEDEC) is responsible for a range of in-service training activities at the secondary level. SEDEC operates through twenty-five secondary education development units at locations, which allow for national coverage.

The training activities also support the work of the Curriculum Development Centre and the OCE.

Janak Educational Materials Centre

The Janak Educational Materials Centre (JEMC), operating as a public limited company, produces and distributes school textbooks throughout Nepal. JEMC's Board of Directors is comprised of representatives from concerned ministries and organizations.

The Curriculum Development Centre

The CDC is responsible for the maintenance, transmission and renewal of the school education curriculum. The wide-ranging activities of the centre include developing, revising and disseminating textbooks and teacher's support materials.

A programme of seminars and workshops supports these activities. CDC's development and monitoring work is carried out by specialized curriculum subject units, advised by curriculum subject specialist committees. Subject units cover languages, science and maths, social studies, health and physical education.

To support CDC's activities, various studies and surveys are conducted on curriculum-related issues and problems. The activities of CDC give rise to a wide range of relationships with other institutions.

The most important of these is with the teachers and student in schools, who are the immediate end-users of the centre's products. CDC also incorporates a publishing unit.

The Publishing Unit (PU)

The PU (in collaboration with subject specialist units, their advisory subject specialist committees, subject advisers and consultants) sets textbook specifications. According to prescribed procedures, the PU also selects textbook writers on the basis of: subject knowledge, classroom experience and sample materials reviewed by teachers/ subject experts.

A PU staff member serves as the managing editor, and is responsible for briefing contracted writers and liaising closely with them to ensure quality and schedule controls, until the camera-ready copy goes to the printers.

The PU manager also arranges distribution of the draft materials to be tested in schools and validated by teacher groups. The managing editor, unit specialist, subject committee members, advisers and specialists all visit schools to collect comments which are subsequently relayed to the writers.

Subject Advisory Committees

The role of these committees is to advise on the preparation and revision of the curriculum, and the preparation, revision and evaluation of textbooks and teachers guides.

The Curriculum Officers, as members of the committees, also participate in these activities and provide the secretariat that promotes the committee's work. Subcommittees are established to carry out specialist developmental inputs. The subject committees cover Nepali, English, science, mathematics, social studies, and health, population and environment (HPE).

Task Committees

Like the publishing unit, the task committees cut across the boundaries of the various specialist units. Examples are the formative assessment committee and the dissemination committee. Task committees are formed to advise the cross-boundary projects managing officer on policy and operational matters.

Implementation and Follow-up of Curriculum Reform

The general aims of secondary education are to: produce healthy citizens who are: familiar with the national tradition, culture, social environment, democratic values; able to use language effectively in daily life; aware of scientific issues; creative, cooperative, industrious; able to contribute to economic development.

The secondary curriculum

The lower secondary curriculum (grades 6, 7 and 8) and the secondary curriculum (grades 9 and 10) are constructed with core subjects and optional subjects. The five lower secondary core subjects are Nepali, English, math, science and social studies.

The six secondary core subjects are Nepali, English, math, science, social studies, health, population and environment (HPE).

A. Option 1 paper subjects (any one)

Languages: Nepali, Arabic, Avadhi, Bhojpuri, Bengalit, Chinese, Hindi, Japanese, Maithili, Sanskrit, Tibetan, Persian, Hebrew, Urdit, English, French, German, Greek, Latin, Russian, Spanish. (Other national languages of Nepal will be included in the curriculum, provided that grammar books, teaching materials, etc., are available.)

Humanities, Social Science: history, geography, civics, economics, sociology.

Optional mathematics

B. Option 2 Paper subjects (any one)

Interdisciplinary: agricultural education, food science, architectural education, industrial education, office management and accounting, auditing, typing and shorthand, computer science, home science, handicrafts painting, sewing and knitting, bamboo-work, dance, music, Ayurveda naturpathy, health and physical education, photography, journalism, instrumentation.

Secondary Education Development Project

The Secondary Education Development Project (SEDP)

began in 1993. SEDP originally aimed at improving and reinforcing three subjects (English, science, mathematics). In 1997, support to Nepali and social studies was added. SEDP also has the goal of reforming the examination system and providing materials and equipment to selected secondary schools. The project has been providing support services through the Secondary Education Development Centre and the twenty-five training centres.

Accomplishments

As of July 1998, CDC had produced ten curriculum booklets outlining the lower secondary curriculum (grades 6-8) and the secondary curriculum (grades 9 and 10) and covering all core subjects therein. The curriculum and textbooks for grades 6 (1996), 7 (1997) and 8 have been printed and distributed (1998). The lower secondary curriculum is being prepared for publication. However, English is the only subject in which teacher's guides have so far been produced.

In July 1998, the National Curriculum Council (NCC) decided to restructure the curriculum of grades 9 and 10, to allow for the inclusion of a new sixth core subject, health, population and environment (HPE). This reduced English, Nepali, mathematics and science from six to five periods each week. The curriculum was adjusted in line with the reduction of periods. The grade 9 production schedule for textbooks and teacher's guides has now been separated from that of grade 10. The grade 9 textbooks for the six core subjects were scheduled for printing by the end of March 1999, while completion of grade 9 teacher's guides was foreseen for the end of April 1999.

CDC has formulated a seven-stage dissemination strategy for the grades 9 and 10 curriculum. The first stage (approval) was completed in November 1998. Included in the strategy are: detailed planning, package development, training of master facilitators and facilitators, training of head-teachers, cluster-based and school-based workshops. The full programme will be completed by the end of July 1999.

The Publishing Unit's first textbooks are clearly of a better quality than previous CDC/SEDP outputs. The unit has also produced a four-page CDC bulletin of a high standard (February 1998) to publicize its activities, as well as a leaflet in English and Nepali. Textbooks have been monitored for gender, socioeconomic and regional equity.

National goals of education

The National Goals of Education frame all the detailed technical work of curriculum development and should be reflected in all documents and materials developed by the Curriculum Development Centre.

The national education goals are to:

— nurture and develop the personalities and inherent talents in each person;

— instill respect for human values and the will to safeguard national and social beliefs so as to help develop a healthy social unity;

— help the individual to socialize, enhancing social unity;

— help the individual keep his or her identity in the national and international context and to help him/her lead a socially harmonious life in the modern world;

— assist the modernization of the country by creating able manpower for its development;

— teach the thoughtful protection and wise use of Nepal's natural resources;

— bring those who are underprivileged into the mainstream of the nation.

Developments and Challenges in the Design, Implementation and follow-up of Curriculum Reform

While the capacity of CDC to handle complex tasks is clearly improving, the capacity to plan and to develop human resources has certain constraints due to the rate of staff changeovers. This makes the institutionalization of curriculum development design processes very difficult. These staff changes are at all professional and administrative levels of the organization.

The same changes create problems of continuity and liaison with other organizations connected with the implementation process. These institutions 'District Education Offices, Regional Education Offices, OCE and SEDEC—also have high staff instability.

There are very few formalized follow-up activities, except by the SEDP BME Unit. These are mainly concerned with project evaluation.

Reforming the Curriculum with special emphasis on social studies

As described earlier all core curricula and many optional subjects have been changed in recent years. In the development of all core curricula there has been tension between traditionalists and modernists, as well as between nationalists and those in favour of globalisation or wider horizons—those who speak for 'our values' and those who speak of 'global values'.

Balancing these diverse views is a problem for all curriculum developers. No curriculum subject can avoid these controversies. While in science and mathematics the debate is narrower, in English and Nepali there are different dimensions due to the source of each individual language. Both of the two newer subjects—social studies and HPE—have proved to be controversial in different ways.

Translating the goals, general objectives and specific objectives of the social studies curriculum into a useful textbook proved difficult. Although there are many dimensions to the discussion, the fundamental debate concerns whether education is about passing knowledge or learning skills—or what is the balance between the two. Members of the subject committee did not always agree with those who set the framework for developing the new textbook, creating what is hopefully a creative tension.

Those setting the framework for developing the new textbook felt that the following factors are all important in the writing of a new style textbook:

— These will include not only factual information for knowledge and understanding, but specific skills such as interpreting a bar chart, locating places of historical importance, presenting an argument in favour of a certain course of action and collecting local data.

— The earlier textbooks mostly contained only factual information, followed by recall questions. The new textbook must present information in different forms (text, statistics, pictures, photographs, diagrams, graphs and charts, maps, newspaper items, source documents) and provide challenging questions to help students understand, interpret, analyse and evaluate the information.

— The textbook must include many project-related activities, starting with simple tasks, and moving towards longer projects. This will mean that most of the work studied has a local component and thus is of genuine relevance to the students. It will also mean that students can experience research activities, gaining practical investigation and analytical skills, and learning to present their findings. It will also help them to work together cooperatively.

— The students should be able to see what skills they are learning in each chapter and gain a sense of achievement and progress towards the school-leaving certificate (SLC). This may be done with a summary of chapters or topics. The exercises given in the textbook will not only test knowledge and understanding, but will expect analysis and evaluation of the information, and well-thought-out answers. They will also need to encourage the practice of practical skills and abilities. This will provide practice for new SLC-type questions.

Social studies curriculum

Objectives

There are twenty-eight general objectives listed in the grades 9 and 10 social studies curricula. Highly specific objectives are listed for grade 9 (twenty-seven objectives) and grade 10 (twenty-nine objectives).

Abilities

On achieving the course objectives, students will be able to demonstrate a wide range of abilities. Some examples of the abilities associated with knowledge and understanding and practical abilities are as follows:

Ability 1: Knowledge and understanding.

1. Describing projects in different zones and development regions;
2. Describing achievements of Nepal in fields of education, health, transportation, telecommunications, electricity and water supply;
3. Discussing the role of skilled manpower in the development of the infrastructure of Nepal;
4. Stating the role of international organizations in solving social problems;
5. Explaining different climates and the elements that affect them;
6. Giving a short introduction to the geo-economic activities of continents;
7. Identifying the problems created by population growth and migration and finding out ways to participate in solving them;

8. Describing the physical features of the Earth;
9. Examining the impact of landslides on the physical features of Nepal and participating in the task of avoiding them;
10. Listing the agricultural products grown in the various geographical areas.

Ability 2: Practical abilities.

1. Maintaining national dignity;
2. Drawing a map of Nepal and filling in the main industrial centres and roads;
3. Demonstrating models in class;
4. Analysing the data presented in charts;
5. Locating historical sites on a map;
6. Investigating the problems of population growth;
7. Appreciating the contributions of our national heroes;
8. Applying the knowledge of social studies for the good of society;
9. Drawing a picture of the Himalayan region;
10. Recording the maximum rainfall of the month;
11. Designing a research proposal to find out about social evils.

Criteria

The new-style social studies textbook must be developed so that students can be thoroughly prepared to take the new SLC examination. The textbook must help them not only to understand the content of the course, but also to develop the necessary skills and ability to think critically about the different topics. Thus, each chapter should have clearly thought-out learning outcomes. These will include not only factual information for knowledge and understanding, but will also include specific skills such as those outlined in the previous section. After studying this lesson the student will be able to:

— interpret a bar chart;

— locate places of historical importance;

— present an argument in favour of a certain course of action;

— collect local data.

The earlier textbooks contained only factual information, followed by recall questions. To prepare for the new SLC examination, the new textbooks must present information in different forms (text, statistics, pictures, photographs, diagrams, graphs and charts, maps, newspaper items, source documents) and provide challenging questions to help students understand, interpret, analyse and evaluate the information. As 30% of the new SLC marks will be given for project-style work to be carried out during the year, the textbook must include many such activities; starting with simple tasks, and evolving to longer projects. This will mean that most of the material studied has a local component and thus is of relevance to the students.

Global Trends in Learning Materials

The World Declaration on Education for All does not contain the words 'textbook' or 'learning materials' and there is only passing reference to such materials in the guidelines for implementation that accompanied the Declaration. Much more attention is given to the potential of technologies newer than print' television, radio and computers. This is not surprising, any more than that a policy declaration on transportation might omit reference to oil or one on television might omit reference to electricity. Schoolbooks have long been considered an essential educational commodity but one that can be turned on or off in supply, much like chalk or desks. It is only in the past decade that the complexities of developing the sustainable provision of books and other learning materials have come to be recognized by funding agencies and, to a lesser extent, by governments. It is only in the 1990s, too, that the importance of all links in the book chain to the sustainable provision of learning materials has come to be appreciated. The value of books, on the other hand, has long been recognized. As early as 1978, Heyneman et al. reported that:

> From the evidence we have so far, the availability of books appears to be the single most consistently positive school factor in predicting academic achievement. In fifteen of the eighteen statistics, it is positive; this is, for example, more favourable than the thirteen out of twenty-four recently reported for teacher training.

In both Nicaragua and the Philippines, for example, testing in the early 1980s found that students with textbooks scored significantly higher, by about one-third of a standard deviation, than students without those resources. In many countries of the developing world, the textbook is the major, if not the only, medium of instruction. It is the main resource for teachers, setting out the general guidelines of the syllabus in concrete form, providing a guide and foundation to the content, order and pacing of instruction, supplying exercises and assignments for students to practise what they have learned. It is both a source of essential information and the basis for examination and appraisal.

The textbook retains its primacy because, in comparison to other educational technologies, books are inexpensive, easy to use, easily portable, and familiar. They can be used in districts where there is no reliable supply of electricity or communication. They can be of particular assistance to the tens of thousands of underqualified and undertrained teachers who have been pressed into service to meet the demands of increasing enrolments throughout the global South. Textbooks, moreover, may be the only introduction to reading for students who come from homes without books. They may be a young persons only exposure to reading in villages so remote that there are no newspapers, magazines or even shop signs. They are essential to teaching literacy in the many parts of the world where book hunger' even book famine' is endemic, where teaching is by rote and memorization of information, not always accurate and seldom up to date. As one expert has remarked, 'on the verge of the second millennium, education transmitted through oracy rather than literacy is inadequate in educating the labour force of a country [Ethiopia] with sixty million people'.

Books are, in short, essential to achieving the goal of Education for All. In large numbers of the world's primary and secondary schools, however, pupils and students have only limited access to them, despite millions of dollars that have been spent on programmes of book provision.

Textbooks cannot stand alone. To be effective, they must be supported by a variety of other educational materials. Each textbook should ideally be accompanied by a teacher's guide to using it.

Such guides may outline innovative ways of teaching a particular lesson, suggest class activities to reinforce the content, and provide examples of exercises and assignments. They are particularly important when a new curriculum or new teaching strategies are being introduced and at all times for inadequately trained teachers.

Supplementary materials expand upon the information in the textbook. They may range from chalk and blackboards to educational television and interactive computerized lessons. Those that are printed reinforce the lessons of literacy taught in the classroom, develop children's ability to read, expand their vocabulary, train them in retrieving and using information, encourage independent reading and may instil a lifelong love of reading and learning.

This survey defines supplementary materials as including work books, reading programmes or schemes, children's fiction (easy readers, stories, plays and anthologies), children's nonfiction, audio tapes, video tapes, multimedia learning packages, science kits, reference books such as dictionaries and atlases, magazines, comics, posters, wall charts and maps.

Most attention will be paid to the supplementary reading materials that may be located in school libraries. When printed supplementary materials are in short supply, as is often the case, it may be assumed that access to electronic materials is even scarcer.

Book provision in 1990

Both the World Declaration on Education for All and its accompanying Framework for Action are concerned with broad policy goals and targets, in only some of which the provision of school books and learning materials play a part.

With respect to that provision, the Framework for Action sets out the following principles:

> 'Addressing the basic learning needs of all means . . . capitalizing on the use of traditional and modern information media and technologies . . . [both of which] need to be designed to ensure equitable access, sustained participation, and effective learning achievement.'
>
> National and subnational planning should cover, among other subjects, 'the basic learning needs to be met . . . the languages to be used in education . . . modalities to mobilize family and local community support; the required capital and recurrent resources . . . possible measures for cost effectiveness, targets and specific objectives, and indicators and procedures to be used to for monitor progress in reaching the targets.'
>
> Attention should be paid to 'reduction of inefficiency in the public sector and exploitative practices in the private sector; provision of improved training for public administrators and of incentives to retain qualified women and men in public service; and provision of

measures to encourage wider participation in the design and implementation of basic education programmes.'

'Efficiency in basic education does not mean providing eduction at the lowest cost, but rather the most effective use of all resources (human, organizational, and financial) to produce the desired levels of access and of necessary learning achievement.'

'Pre- and in-service training programmes for key personnel should be initiated, or strengthened where they do exist.' [In this context, curriculum developers are mentioned, but not publishing professionalism.]

'The quality and delivery of basic education can be enhanced through the judicious use of instructional technologies . . . (educational radio and television, computers, and audiovisual instructional devices) [which over time will] become less expensive and more adaptable to a range of environments.'

'Existing regional partnerships will need to be strengthened and provided with the resources necessary for their effective functioning in helping countries meet the basic learning needs of their populations.'

Textbook availability Most governments, and most educators, would like to provide every pupil with a complete set of school books in every subject, free of charge.

That, at least, is the ideal target' a text-book: pupil ratio of 1:1. In fact, it is a target imported from the industrialized nations that may be unnecessarily expensive.

An often-quoted experiment in the Philippines suggests that when school books are the property of the school and are not taken home, there is only a marginal difference between ratios of 1:1 and 1:2, and some experts have suggested that a ratio of 1:3 should be regarded as satisfactory.

Very few countries outside the industrialized North could afford to reach even the lowest of these targets in 1990. Instead, as a result of global recession and rising enrolments, the standard of textbook provision deteriorated during the late 1970s and the 1980s throughout Africa and in much of Latin America and Asia. It was well below the ideal as the decade came to a close.

A survey in 1990-91 of Bolivia, Colombia, Chile, Ecuador, Panama, Peru and Venezuela found that only 32 per cent of pupils between Grades 1 and 5 had textbooks; variations between countries ranged from 64 per cent in Chile to 20 per cent or less in Ecuador, Peru and Venezuela.

In Mexico, the figure rose to 75 per cent thanks to a national textbook programme; in Brazil, it was estimated at about 33 per cent. The national averages mask serious variations.

In general, book provision was much better in the cities and towns than in rural areas, and areas that were difficult to reach had the fewest books' sometimes none. The pattern of rural deprivation has been most clearly documented in Africa.

A summary of book sector studies in eight African countries found satisfactory to good ratios in the elite schools in important urban areas, but generally low levels of textbook provision at the primary level. Angola, Kenya, Nigeria and the United Republic of Tanzania recorded primary- level textbook:pupil ratios of 2:3 or better in urban areas, but 1:20 or worse elsewhere.

In Nigeria, the situation grew notably worse as one travelled northwards; in the majority of schools visited during a book sector study, the text-book: pupil ratio was 1:10 and sometimes 1:100. In the United Republic of Tanzania, a primary-level mathematics book that was available at a 1:3 ratio in the Southern Highlands plummeted to 1:700 in the Lake zone.

Only Sierra Leone had achieved a broad equity of supply between rural and urban areas, at a ratio of 1:3, as a result of an externally funded text-book project that paid particular attention to distribution networks. (Before the project, the ratio in Sierra Leone was close to 1:1,000.)

At the secondary level, few books were available in Angola, the United Republic of Tanzania or Zambia; in Kenya, Nigeria and Sierra Leone the ratios were between 1:10 and 1:28, implying only one to four textbooks per class.

Elite secondary schools, once again, were likely to have more textbooks. Most of the textbooks in the secondary schools had been repaired and maintained for fifteen to twenty years.

Variations between subjects and grades have also been noted. In Burundi, books were available only for language arts subjects in French and Kirundi.

The SECAB survey of Grades 1 to 5 in six South American countries found that while 70 per cent of the students had textbooks in Spanish language, only 30 per cent had textbooks in mathematics and fewer than 10 per cent had them in science and social science.

Where books were provided free of charge, those for a particular subject or grade were often unavailable when needed because of delays in printing and distribution. Where books were sold, variations reflected parental priorities and incomes. Parents were more likely to buy books in subjects that would contribute to their child's future financial success. In provinces of China where rural schools had little in the way of state-provided learning resources and parents bought books, teachers in the poorest areas sometimes bought books for children from their own salaries.

At the tertiary level, textbooks in Africa and many other countries were in chronically short supply. A great majority were imported and had become prohibitively expensive, despite schemes sponsored by the British and French governments to supply special low-cost editions. Shortages were more serious in teacher training and vocational institutes than in universities.

The translation of broad curriculum outlines to a concrete book is no simple task. The book must be written at a level of concept, content and vocabulary that is appropriate for the majority of pupils at the grade level and in a way that, ideally, will interest and motivate them. It must be consistent in approach, method and explanation. It should be of use to the less-qualified teacher but allow the good teacher to expand upon its content. Writing a good textbook requires the skills of a subject specialist, a curriculum expert, a good teacher with classroom experience and an imaginative author; the writing of such books is increasingly a team effort.

In 1990 there was ample evidence that the books used in schools in many parts of the world fell below these standards. They suffered from poor instructional design, particularly in the scope and sequence of material. A study of textbooks for Grades 1, 3, and 5 in fifteen countries found that for the earlier grades the material in mathematics and reading was too difficult; in Grade 5, the mathematics books were also too difficult but the reading books would have been more suitable for students in Grades 2 and 3. Textbooks in Pakistan were characterized by poor language grading from one level to another and even between subjects at the same level; teachers said the books were overly difficult for their students. Difficult books in the early grades were seen as contributing to the high early dropout rate in many countries. A study of textbooks in Mozambique found that, while they followed the established curriculum, they were generally too theoretical and lacked sufficient linkages to the everyday experiences of the target users. Neumann quoted a Deputy Minister of Education in the Philippines as saying that textbooks in his country should be aimed towards the schools in poor villages; nevertheless, most of the officially approved school books in the 1980s catered for the urban élite.

Textbooks also suffered from errors in fact and grammar, inappropriate illustrations and a poor choice of language or script. In many of the African countries, books were written in English, French or Portuguese, even though in any one country fewer than 20 per cent of the population was likely to be literate in any one of these metropolitan languages. Textbooks in the republics of the former Union of Soviet Socialist Republics were in Russian, ignoring local languages such as Azeri, Turkmen, Kazakh, Uzbek and Kyrgyz. In Pakistan, children could not read fluently the Arabic-style Nasakh script favoured by the curriculum developers and textbook writers, and as a result depended on their teachers to read the books for them and summarize the lessons.

In text and illustration, the books tended to reinforce traditional views of men and women. Lockheed and Verspoor et al., cite various studies showing girls or women in passive roles. A primary-school book in Swaziland depicted a boy happily playing ball and a girl shying away from a snake. In the twenty-nine most widely used primary textbooks in Peru, three-quarters of all references to and illustrations of people were of men. Similar discrepancies characterized the representation of men and women in school books from Costa Rica, Egypt, Kuwait, Lebanon, Qatar, Saudi Arabia, Tunisia, Yemen and Zambia. There were signs of change. In Costa Rica, after new books were produced with support from the United States Agency for International Co-operation (USAID), the proportion of women and girls in illustrations rose from 25 per cent to 31 per cent; female figures no longer were shown as less independent and more often in stereotypically male roles; males were sometimes shown as caring for children or undertaking domestic tasks.

To an increasing extent, even in former colonial countries, text-books were being written by local experts. European books were no longer being adapted, and even transnational publishers were using local authors with local teaching experience. If the books were less perfect pedagogically than their Northern counterparts, they were less Eurocentric and thus more related to the experience of pupils. In most countries, the physical quality of the books was well below Northern standards. Imported paper was expensive, binding facilities limited, and machinery old and in need of repair. As a result, books were too often poorly printed on low-grade paper, inadequately bound by the adhesive ('perfect') method, and used only black and white illustrations of varying quality. Such books could not stand up to the rigours of rainy climates, when pupils often had to walk long distances between home and school. Everywhere, the perfect-bound books were apt to fall apart. Externally funded textbook projects often used better paper and their products could be expected to last three years or more. Some incorporated four-colour printing, a feature that might be difficult to retain after the project closed. The number of subjects, and therefore the number of textbooks, was increasing in some countries. This trend was evident in Africa, where it was increasing strains on budgets and teachers.

In most cases, however, only core subjects were actually available, and some countries were reversing the trend. Mozambique, for example, had decided to concentrate on six core subjects for Grade 5 as opposed to the eleven subjects then taught in The United Republic of Tanzania. Ethiopia had decided to teach three subjects (natural and exact sciences, and geography) as environmental studies, with a single textbook.

Statistics of textbook provision are notoriously unreliable. Books that are reported to have been produced do not always reach the schools. They may be damaged in transit, pilfered or, more commonly, held up in district storehouses for lack of resources to carry them further. Those that reach the schools, moreover, may not be used in the classroom. This was apparently often the case in 1990.

The reasons for non-use varied. In some countries, government regulations made ill-paid teachers responsible for replacing lost and damaged books, and as a result teachers kept the books locked up. Teachers were not trained in the methods of new textbooks and therefore hesitated to use them or were reluctant to use them because their interests and experiences, and those of their students, were not reflected in the content. Some teachers felt threatened by new textbooks, and there was some evidence that less experienced teachers, who might be expected to benefit most from a carefully prepared textbook, were less likely to use them than were their more experienced colleagues.

Teachers' guides were seldom available in developing countries. Lockheed and Verspoor cite various studies: schools in Guinea-Bissau had guides only for Grade 1; in Malawi, fewer than 15 per cent of teachers had received a guide for a subject other than English; in rural Brazil, only 44 per cent of teachers had received teachers' guides. Where textbooks were bought by parents rather than provided by the state, teachers' guides were apt to be in particularly short supply. Moreover, many guides were unrelated to the ability of the average classroom teacher and were often designed without consideration of the teacher's reading fluency or the conditions under which the guides would be read; small type, for example, was ill-suited to be read in the poor lighting of rural communities.

Where textbooks were in short supply, supplementary materials might be expected to be even more scarce. In many countries school libraries either did not exist or had fallen into disrepair at the primary and secondary levels, except in elite public or private schools. Book stocks were outdated, and very often Eurocentric. At the tertiary level, textbooks and reference works were so scarce that students resorted to wholesale photocopying of library titles, if not to theft or mutilation. Even university libraries that had been well stocked in the past had been unable to buy many new books or journals for some years. Public libraries, a resource for school children, also deteriorated, although Mexico was remarkable in creating some 3,500 new public libraries in the period 1982-92 in a national system that served 71 million readers stretching from the capital to remote villages isolated by mountains, rivers and jungle.

In nine African countries surveyed in book sector studies, libraries and supplementary materials were seriously underfunded as governments channelled scarce resources primarily into textbooks. The majority of primary and secondary schoolchildren had no access to books or other reading materials apart from textbooks. Most books that were available were European in origin and inappropriate in content. There were not enough books about African history, geography, literature or cultures. Teachers and principals were not trained in the maintenance and use of school libraries. At secondary level, school libraries were disintegrating in terms of stock, buildings, furniture and trained staff. In some countries, governments distributed supplementary reading materials to the schools but did not develop the infrastructure to store and use them. Sierra Leone, however, did take that important basic step and, as a result, supplementary materials it had distributed to the schools five years earlier were still in place.

Schools that did have supplementary materials performed better than those that did not. The Escuela Nueva programme in Colombia used a variety of instructional materials, including school libraries, to great effect.

High achieving schools in Thailand benefited from community support for the purchase of supplementary text materials. Supplementary materials were also reported to have been used successfully at the Gonakelle school in Sri Lanka and in adult literacy programmes in Nepal.

Methods of textbook provision

Pupils in public systems of education received textbooks in one of three ways.

1. *Provided free of charge by the state.* This was the method followed in many countries of Asia, Africa, Latin America and the socialist republics of eastern Europe and western Asia. Free provision was more common in primary schools than at the secondary level. Books might be produced cheaply and given to the pupils each year for them to keep (as in the soviet republics) or given to the schools and lent to the pupils for their use during the school year on the understanding that they would be returned.

The provision of free books was intended to ensure equity in availability (although it did not) and responded to a viewpoint expressed by one Mexican expert that' if a government says that elementary education becomes an obligation for every citizen, then the government should provide the facilities for such education.' Remarkably, in some African countries university students were given free tuition and free books but primary school students were expected to pay for books, thus reinforcing an elite at the expense of the broader population.

2. *Sold through commercial channels.* Parents or students bought books, usually through retail outlets. The price of books might be subsidized by the state, sometimes with external assistance. Textbooks were sold at the primary level in some countries of Africa, Asia, and Latin America and the Caribbean. In the newly industrialized countries of Asia, textbooks were generally published by privately owned companies that worked closely with the educational authorities but usually received only limited assistance or subsidy from the government. Practices could vary within a single country: in Nigeria, primary-level textbooks were free in the Northern states but sold in the Southern and Eastern states.

Selling the book inevitably led to inequities. First, bookstores were located primarily in the urban centres, although text-books (a short-term investment with rapid turnover) might be sold at the beginning of the school year in stationery shops and other small retail outlets elsewhere. In the primarily rural Northwest Frontier Province of Pakistan, for example, text-books produced by the provincial textbook board were sold through a network of wholesale distributors and retailers that stretched from the provincial capital into the villages. Second, not all parents could afford to buy textbooks for their children. In Côte d'Ivoire, a textbook cost about one-tenth of the monthly salary of the head of an average family. Where books were in particularly short supply, as in Angola, a black market operated with high markups. Third, textbooks might not be available when needed because of inef-9 Thematic Studies Textbooks and Learning Materials 1990-99. Efficient ordering by the retailers or delays in shipping, which could be especially serious in a country or region with many islands, such as the Philippines or eastern Caribbean.

3. *Book rental.* Under this method, a school bought or was given class sets or part class sets of books and issued the books to the pupils in return for an annual fee. The books would be returned at the end of the year for reuse. The fee was set to recover part or all of the cost of replacing the books and to that end the rental income was placed in a revolving fund. This method allowed educational authorities to amortize the cost of books over a three- to five-year period, depending on the anticipated life of the textbook, and thus reduce the annual cost to the pupils or their parents. Such a system had been operating successfully in Lesotho for eight years, despite some problems, including delinquency in payments and inaccurate projections of needs. The government was planning, however, to supplement rental fees with an annual allocation to cover the costs of distribution and administratio. Rental schemes were seen as particularly desirable at the secondary level, but could operate in primary and tertiary institutions. In a variation on such schemes, parents might be required to supplement government allocations. In

> Fiji, for example, because a flat grant from the Ministry of Education for each enrolled pupil was not large enough to cover full operating costs, some school committees charged parents a small sum for the purchase of textbooks, library books, and other materials.

In private schools, students would normally be expected to buy textbooks, which might or might not be the same as those used in the public system.

Production of textbooks

Historically, the provision of textbooks in developing countries followed three stages. Initially, the countries imported existing books from the North, usually from the colonial or former colonial power. Next, they began using adapted versions of foreign books, modified to meet local needs and experience, and often published by transnational companies based in the former colonial power. In the third stage, books were written and produced locally, often by the state.

By 1990 most countries had achieved local production, at least of primary-school textbooks, although specialized secondary-school textbooks were more likely to be adapted and tertiary texts often were imported. Typically, each country sought to produce its own books, sometimes without taking advantage of possible adaptations that would benefit from investments already made by other publishers in developing instructional methods. International trade in textbooks, either as licensing of adaptations or as imports of finished books, generally followed the path of North to South from the metropolitan countries of Europe and North America . To support local production, some countries imposed regulatory barriers. Zimbabwe, which secured its books entirely from the private sector, required local reprinting of foreign-originated books that sold more than 5,000 copies, and indeed began exporting text-books to neighbouring countries.

Local production was common even in sub-Saharan Africa, where large-scale book production was still relatively new and where the shortage of books was so acute that Hans Zell, the principal chronicler of African publishing, could exclaim that 'The picture of Africa at the end of the 1980s is largely that of a bookless society.'

In English-speaking sub-Saharan Africa, British transnationals (notably Macmillan, Heinemann, Oxford and Longman) had established sales offices which, in the more populated countries, functioned as regional publishers. As a result of the economic recession of the 1980s, many of these transnational branches closed, leaving behind trained editors and other staff who were ready to begin their own enterprises. By 1990 several branches had passed to private local ownership or control (for example, in Kenya and Nigeria). Elsewhere, foreign publishers entered into joint ventures with locally owned publishers of textbooks, which were often parastatal organizations in which the state retained a controlling share. Namibia, unlike other English-speaking countries of Africa, still depended primarily on imports, in its case from South Africa.

The countries of French-speaking Africa still imported large quantities of textbooks from France. In 1987, French-speaking Africa, excluding the Magreb, represented 13 per cent of the export market for French books, even though prices there averaged 44 per cent more than those in other French export markets that benefited from cheaper insurance and shipping, and lower risk. In 1990, ten countries of French-speaking Africa imported FF 163.7 million worth of books from France; in six of the ten, textbooks accounted for almost two-thirds of the total book imports; in the other four, where Arabic was a significant language, the textbook proportion shrank to 36 per cent. French publishers also had stakes in locally controlled textbook publishing houses. Local print runs could be substantial: le Centre d'édition et distribution africain (CEDA), owned jointly by the government of Côte d'Ivoire and the French publisher Hatier, printed 250,000 copies of one textbook.

Regional co-operation in publishing was rare. The ministries of education of eight French-speaking countries of sub-Saharan Africa, however, began the process in 1988 by identifying core subjects, such as French, mathematics and science, in which they could develop common curricula and textbooks. By 1990 they were well under way to producing the first books in mathematics.

In both English- and French-speaking Africa, state-owned and parastatal publishers benefited from hidden subsidies (for example, rent and staff costs that did not need to be recovered from sales, tax exemptions on supplies, subsidized state-owned or parastatal printing). Locally owned private publishers occasionally ventured into the school market, but for the most part they were marginalized by the much larger transactional, foreign, state-owned or parastatal textbook publishing operations.

In virtually every country of the world, the state is involved to some extent in the provision of learning materials' at the very least by establishing the curricula on which school books are based and, even in the freest of markets, by buying some or all of the materials used in the public system. In most of the world outside Western Europe and North America, the state played a much greater role than that in 1990. In many countries, the same Ministry of Education unit that defined the curriculum was also responsible for writing the books to support it. School books were printed in plants that were owned by governments or parastatals. Books were published by the Ministry or by parastatals under its control. Distribution also was often the responsibility of the Ministry or a parastatal. In some countries, particularly those with communist or strongly socialist governments, the entire process' from writing to use in the schools' was carried out by government ministries or agencies. In the former USSR, for example, all curricular materials were designed, controlled, manufactured and distributed free of charge, in sufficient quantities, by the state; the republics all had a uniform supply of such materials and followed the same curricula. In other countries the private sector might be involved in one stage or more of textbook provision. However, even in some countries with large commercial publishing industries, such as India, the state might retain responsibility for publishing textbooks for the public system. Searle listed possible combinations of private and state engagement and showed how functional responsibilities were divided in twenty-five countries where the World Bank had financed projects that had textbook provision as a component. Almost all the projects were in four regions: Eastern Africa, Western Africa, Latin America and the Caribbean, and East Asia and the Pacific. The diversity of patterns was remarkable. For the twenty-five countries examined, there were nineteen different patterns or arrangements of the four aspects of textbook provision considered. Only two patterns recurred.

State predominance was more evident in the ten African countries surveyed by Brunswic and Hajjar (1992). In most of the countries of French-speaking Africa, a specialized institution (commonly called l'Institut pédagogique national) was responsible for developing editorial guidelines, preparing manuscripts, and commissioning, publishing, printing and/or approving textbooks. In Senegal and Togo, the Ministry of Education had direct responsibility.

In some countries, state involvement in the provision of learning materials, as in other parts of the economy, was a matter of ideology. In others it began as a response to perceived necessity. With independence, former colonies had no indigenous source of school books. Foreign publishers who had supplied textbooks in the past were suspect as agents of colonialism and were themselves wary of investing in or extending credit to the newly independent countries. Yet there was an immediate need, not only in the former colonies but everywhere in the developing world, for cheap books to educate growing populations in curricula that had been revised to meet new national conditions and aspirations, and at the higher level to meet the demand for trained professionals and public servants. The private sector of most countries did not have the infrastructure or the capital to meet this challenge, and most families did not have the money to buy commercially produced books at full cost. Very small countries, such as the island states of the South Pacific, had no alternative to state responsibility. The task was taken on by government, if not from political belief, by default.

Tabel 2: Functional responsibilities in ten African countries with respect to textbooks

	Ministry of education or other government agency	State and private	Private sector
Writing	8	1	1
Production	6	3	1
Distribution	6	1	3
Financing	2	4	4

State involvement was seen as a means of controlling the use of scarce resources and subsidies. It was believed to be economical because it eliminated the markups and profit of commercial printing, publishing and bookselling. The Ministry could determine quantities and schedules, and ensure they were met. Those transnational publishers who continued to do business in developing countries were not averse to working with governments, particularly if in that way they could secure a monopoly or dominant position in providing textbooks. The World Bank and other major bilateral donors also worked with governments as a matter of policy, and in two early large projects in the Philippines and Indonesia (and in others later) encouraged the development of a central agency to develop, produce and distribute textbooks. A study sponsored by the World Bank concluded that:

> Developing sustainable capacity for creating, testing, producing, and distributing student learning materials' as well as teacher guides and in-service training materials' requires a significant commitment of the central ministry's resources. Experience in Bangladesh, China, Ethiopia, and the Philippines suggests that textbook

agencies, whether autonomous or divisions of the (national or federal) eduction ministry, are essential to establishing and sustaining a program of materials development. . . . Even small countries, where publishing industries are relatively weak because the market for textbooks is small, may have to set up a clearly defined unit for developing instructional materials, carrying out the design, development, and testing necessary to achieve high quality, and managing the storage and distribution of materials.

The dominance of the state impeded the development of private-sector educational publishing, and thus perpetuated the need for state involvement in countries where it existed. It also nurtured a 'state provider' mentality that proved difficult to dislodge.

Problems commonly ascribed to government bureaucracies arose. Policies changed and so did ministers. One major textbook project dealt with eight ministers of education in four years, each with a new approach to policy. Civil servants were often poorly motivated to seek economies and usually inexperienced in publishing practices. In many countries they were posted in and out of positions without regard to continuity, at the sacrifice of institutional memory. There was wastage and inefficiency, and some corruption' unsurprising when civil service wages fell far below the cost of living. There was inadequate co-ordination among the various functions of writing, production and distribution. An adviser to the World Bank warned that when government agencies produced textbook manuscripts for publication, the procedure was fraught with political implications and conflict of interest. Some of these problems bedeviled similar experiments everywhere. In Sweden, for example, a huge state-owned publishing house had collapsed under the weight of a large bureaucracy and great financial losses.

Separate state-owned companies, or parastatals, were created in an effort to retain government control without some of the constraints of government personnel policies. They were given considerable managerial and financial autonomy but received funds and sometimes direction from the government. It was expected that they would be managed more in line with commercial publishing practices. Some parastatals were joint ventures between the government and one or more foreign commercial publishers. CEDA, previously mentioned, in which the Ivorian government held 51 per cent, was one such venture, as was Nouvelles éditions africaines, which, before its breakup into three national companies in 1988, was owned jointly by the governments of Senegal, Côte d'Ivoire and Togo (60 per cent), and a consortium of French firms, and became a major force in publishing with a long list of titles. In English-speaking Africa, British publishers entered into joint ventures with parastatals in Ghana, the United Republic of Tanzania and Uganda, experiments which Buchan characterized as 'interesting and desirable . . . but too often the interests of overseas commercial publisher and local state enterprise were too divergent for them to stay together.'

In countries where the government dominated the writing and publishing of learning materials, there was normally only one textbook for each subject/level. This was the case in countries that required a massive effort simply to produce the single text in sufficient numbers, such as the Philippines and Indonesia, in the socialist countries of Asia and eastern Europe, in the USSR, and in many countries of Africa. In countries that permitted private-sector educational publishing, there might be a choice among competing textbooks, although in some cases the market was dominated by a single publishing house, local or foreign-owned. Zimbabwe and Nigeria were among the few African nations that permitted multiple choice in an open market in which schools chose the texts they would use from a list of government-approved titles.

Constraints in provision

Educational publishers, whether state-controlled or privately owned, faced serious constraints in 1990. The most important were in financing, production, distribution, information and human resources.

Financing. Book publishing of any kind, but especially the publishing of textbooks, is a capital-intensive business. It typically takes three years to identify authors, plan and write a textbook, edit it, pretest it in classrooms, prepare it for printing, print and bind it, and deliver it to the schools. With luck, the process may take less time, but more often it takes longer. During this time, staff and office expenses must be paid, paper and other materials bought and printers paid. A competitive textbook market involves additional expenses for marketing and promotion. If the books are to be sold, it may take two to three years more to recoup the capital investment.

The global recession of the 1980s and the policies of structural adjustment had a devastating effect on government budgets for education, especially on non-salary items such as books. Between 1985 and 1990, real public expenditure per pupil fell at the primary level in seven of nine Latin American countries for which data were available and in thirteen of twenty in Africa; it also fell at the secondary level in Africa. Budgets for classroom resources (books, teaching aids, furniture and other equipment) were already low.

When industrial countries were allocating 14 per cent of primary-school recurrent costs to classroom resources and 86 per cent to salaries, Asian countries were allocating 9 per cent to classroom resources and African countries only 4 per cent. Expenditures on learning materials and other non-salary recurrent expenses fell in countries suffering from recession, sometimes to close to zero. Supplementary materials were the first to be affected, then textbooks. The reduction in learning material procurement may have slowed after the middle of the decade, but only because by then salaries accounted for almost all recurrent expenditures. The trend was felt most strongly in sub-Saharan Africa. There, expenditure on educational materials represented about 1 per cent of the recurrent primary school budget in 1983, the equivalent of about US$0.60 per pupil. Given the unequal distribution of books, rural areas suffered disproportionately.

Within this restricted market, educational publishers in the private sector faced an additional hurdle: finding credit to capitalize textbook projects. Interest rates rose under structural adjustment, in some countries to 40 per cent or more. Banks, moreover, were reluctant to lend money to entrepreneurs in a high-risk, low-profit industry, or to recognize books in the warehouse or work in progress as collateral. Paper ceases to be collateral as soon as it is printed upon.

Under the stringency of falling export revenues, devaluation, inflation, and structural adjustment, African governments increased efforts to achieve partial or full recovery of costs in textbooks. Lesotho's success has already been mentioned. Ethiopia began charging for textbooks lent for the school year, with 45 per cent of the revenue being retained for printing more books and the balance shared between the schools and the regional offices; the latter was expected to use its share for expanding school library facilities. Angola and Mozambique sold textbooks but subsidized the price substantially. Uganda experimented with a subsidized rental fee.

Partial cost recovery, of course, did no more than reduce the problem of budget shortages. It did not make a nation's educational publishing programme financially self-sustaining. In Ghana, for example, a long-established system of partial cost recovery collapsed because revenue was insufficient to maintain supply. Under new guidelines issued in 1987, textbooks were to be rented for a fee that was based on the cost of production and the expected life span of the books.

For many countries, cost recovery was a new approach beset with problems. In Paraguay, for example, a government scheme to sell textbooks for profit through its Internal Revenue Service offices foundered and 90 per cent of the books were unsold. More commonly, books were unknowingly sold below true cost because of inadequate bookkeeping in Ministry or parastatal offices. In 1986 a World Bank publication suggested a radically different approach' one that would be relatively easy to administer if politically difficult' for cost recovery in one sector to benefit another.

The authors proposed that governments eliminate the free tuition and living allowances then commonly paid to African university students (a practice that reinforced an already existing elite) and invest the money thus saved in primary education. They calculated that if twelve African countries were to eliminate living allowances, the public resources thus freed would allow, on average, an 18 per cent expansion in the yearly budget for primary education. Nationally, the figure ranged from just under 3 per cent in Sudan to more than 40 per cent in Togo. If fees were introduced to cover all the operating costs of higher education, an additional expansion of 22.5 per cent in primary education would be possible.

Single most expensive item in book production costs, representing between 45 and 70 per cent of the cost of manufacture. Most of the paper suitable for books was produced in the North, and prices were set by demand from the prime user, the United States. Countries that had developed their own paper-making capacity often protected it with high tariffs, even for educational purposes, and locally produced paper was sometimes more expensive than superior stock produced overseas.

Book printing is specialized work, different in its requirements from printing newspapers, magazines or other commercial products. Capacity was limited by the number of book printers in most countries and by the quality of their equipment. Costs were driven up when presses and other machinery were old and ill-maintained, occasioning frequent need for repairs and consequent down time. Paper was misappropriated, damaged in transit, or used inefficiently because of mismatches between available sheet sizes and the printer's press size. A publisher in one developing country suggested that paper wastage from mismatching could reach as high as 50 per cent. Books were also delayed by mismatches in equipment' most commonly between new high-speed presses and outdated binding technology. The shortage of thread-binding equipment forced dependence on adhesive binding and resulted in books that fell apart. Printing and binding machinery, spare parts and materials were subject to high duties and sales taxes. Under such conditions, quality suffered, as did prices and schedules.

Local control of publishing does not require local printing. Commercial publishers in the North commonly crossed oceans in search of the most cost-effective printing. Many governments in the South, however, insisted that books be printed at home, often in state-owned or parastatal plants, regardless of efficiency or cost. In three of nine African countries surveyed in book sector studies, local printing prices were higher than could be obtained outside the country. Donated printing equipment not infrequently sat gathering dust for lack of trained operators or because there was no local service agency to repair it. Some equipment stood idle for much of the year because its capacity was far greater than needed.

Distribution. Geography impedes distribution in much of the global South. Some countries are archipelagos' there are 10,000 islands in Indonesia and 7,000 in the Philippines' or are themselves islands, separated by ocean from their neighbours. Transport is impeded by rivers, mountains, deserts and jungles. Roads are poor and trucking often inadequate. Tens of thousands of schools are hours from the nearest road and books for them must be delivered by canoe, head porterage or pack animal. State-supported distribution systems generally depended on teachers, parents or the community to carry learning materials from district depots to isolated schools. Even that system was seen to be breaking down as teachers' salaries dropped in real terms and were paid less reliably.

Where the state was responsible for distribution, books typically were gathered in a central warehouse and shipped to district depots, whence they were directed to schools. In some countries there was an additional step, books going first to regional depots, to be divided there for transshipment to districts and thence to schools. At each stage, there was the possibility of failure. District offices often lacked the funds to pay forwarders, sometimes because the money had not been provided, sometimes because they had never accounted properly for the previous year's advance for that purpose. Packaging and storage were often inadequate to protect the books against water, insects, mould and vermin. In one instance during the rainy season in 1984, new books were delivered to a regional store in Ghana that had no roof; within days the books were soaked and useless.

Books could be delayed by erratic shipping schedules or by the pursuit of economies. In order to ship books efficiently orders were often consolidated, in which case the total order could be held up until the last title was delivered by the printer or publisher. Sometimes distribution costs were unnecessarily high: in the scattered islands of the eastern Caribbean, for example, textbooks were sometimes delivered by freighter or even more expensive air freight, despite the presence of a regular, reliable and inexpensive domestic service that provided baking flour to the islands by boat.

Efficient, economical distribution was further impeded by a lack of adequate information from the schools. Depot storekeepers were untrained in inventory control and maintenance. Books were damaged, lost or stolen. A combination of delays, from development through to distribution, could result in books being delivered a year, or even three years, behind schedule.

In most countries where books were sold through retail outlets, bookstores were scarce in the urban centres and almost unknown outside the cities. Distribution depended on an informal network of suppliers.

Information. Efficient provision requires accurate and timely information on which to project enrolments, and therefore textbook needs, by school, grade and subject. Central planners need data on the number, size and type of schools; current enrolments by grade, school, sex and age; historical and projected rates of change in enrolment; numbers of teachers; numbers of school libraries; and so on. This kind of information was difficult to accumulate in countries where communication by telephone or mail was unreliable. Data were incomplete, sometimes false, more often outdated and pitted with errors created during collation at several steps up the ladder to the central office.

Human resources. Ministry of Education staff were rarely familiar with printing and publishing practices. Curriculum developers were often expected to make major decisions with little or no idea about the implications in cost or time involved. Costs were inflated by ill-informed decisions about book length, illustrations, colours and format.

Government, parastatal and private-sector publishers all suffered from a lack of trained personnel' authors, editors, evaluators, designers, production co-ordinators, distribution and warehouse supervisors, financial and publishing managers. Some publishing institutions obtained training through partnership with overseas commercial publishers. Others sent staff to short-term training courses within Africa or for long-term training abroad, but these resources in 1990 were still relatively limited.

To fund the growing needs of education, governments looked for international help. The World Bank expanded its mandate from project-related vocational training to provide support for school buildings, textbooks, curriculum development and institutional development. The proportion of education projects with textbook components grew steadily, from about 6 per cent before 1974 to 32 per cent in 1979-83 to almost 65 per cent by 1990. In northeast Brazil, a Bank project tripled the number of students receiving textbooks; in the Philippines, a massive effort was funded to reduce the textbook:pupil ratio from 1:10 to 1:2. In three projects alone, in the Philippines, Indonesia, and Ethiopia, more than 350 million textbooks were produced. The process was not without growing pains, however, as Barbara Searle recognized in a review of the Bank's educational projects over the previous ten years. She identified serious shortcomings:

> This review makes it clear that at least some of the projects approved early in this decade recognized that textbook publishing is complex and highly technical; that it requires professional competence in many specialties; and that developing a good textbook takes time, three years at a minimum. Yet, even with this recognition, projects underestimated the difficulties. Of the nine projects surveyed, only

> three . . . left behind functioning textbook provision schemes. Beyond this, the completed projects provide evidence for shortfalls in every aspect of textbook provision: poor quality books, inadequate distribution systems, inability to establish and maintain production schedules, inadequate procedures for handling paper procurement, teacher training activities out of phase with book publication, poor co-ordination between curriculum and manuscript development, and, above all, failure to establish institutions that can continue to provide good quality books after project completion.

Some 90 per cent of the forty-eight projects she reviewed financed the purchase or printing of textbooks, but fewer than half included teacher training, monitoring and evaluation, or dealt with policy changes. Only half the projects that provided books also financed manuscript development and book distribution, and only half of those (eleven projects) also financed teacher training. Only ten projects explicitly dealt with the institutional structure of the textbook provision system and modified it in some way. She concluded that:

> the likelihood of a textbook component attaining its objectives is directly related to the extent to which the project design addresses all aspects of the textbook provision system. It is not crucial that a project finance every component. However, the analysis of the system that is undertaken during preparation and appraisal must include all aspects to make sure that the entire supporting system is in place and functioning well.

The World Bank was the leading, but not the only international, agency supporting textbook provision. The British Overseas Development Administration had textbook programmes in Sierra, Leone, Jamaica and

Jordan. Its three-year project in Sierra Leone, where there was no publishing capacity when financing began in 1984, extended beyond book provision to creation of school storage and a school management system, teacher training in a new curriculum and use of textbooks, warehouse improvement and training of publishing staff. In French-speaking Africa, l'Agence de coopération culturelle et technique (ACCT), supported by France, Canada and Belgium, distributed dictionaries and reading materials to schools and in 1990 was organizing a training programme in printing, publishing, book distribution and bookstore management. Scandinavian governments were notable for their support of book development. The Swedish International Development Co-operation Agency (Sida) was active in Bangladesh, Cambodia, Ethiopia, Guinea-Bissau, Mozambique, the United Republic of Tanzania and Zambia; the Finnish International Development Agency (FINNIDA), in Namibia and Zambia; and Danish International Development Assistance (Danida), in Burkina Faso, Nepal, Uganda, the United Republic of Tanzania, and Zimbabwe. Non-governmental organizations, often with funding from their national government's aid agency, played a small but increasing role as well. The Canadian Organization for Development through Education (CODE), for example, supplied paper and distributed supplementary materials, and several book-related organizations in Europe organized short training courses.

The smaller contributions were generally ad hoc, uncoordinated, and short-term. Individual agencies had their own agendas, political or altruistic. Several projects involved the supply of paper, a short-term solution to immediate needs that could have the longer-term effect of distorting the market. (Unless the equivalent cost of the donated paper was recognized when it was used, book prices would rise abruptly when the supply ended and paper had again to be bought on the market. Then fiscal allocations for textbooks would have to be increased or, more often, textbook provision sharply reduced.) Equipment was too often supplied without spare parts or technical support for maintenance and repair. One-time seminars and workshops were held for writers, editors, publishers, printers and booksellers, but with little or no follow-up, and funding agencies were sometimes disappointed to find that people, once trained, moved from school book publishing to better paying jobs. Funders complained that they had difficulty in identifying all the links in the publishing chain and in understanding the broad concerns that underlay what might seem a simple project. The impact of much of the effort was short-lived and local.

One major exception was a loan guarantee scheme started in Kenya by the Dag Hammarskjøld Foundation, with support from the Ford Foundation of US$300,000. The Foundation negotiated with local banks to guarantee credit extended to local publishers in a normal way. Kenya was chosen because it had a well-developed book market, but one then dominated by transnational publishers. Eleven applications for loans were accepted under the scheme. There were problems in communication' the banks initially expected to be repaid as soon as books were published, not understanding that it takes time to recover publishing costs through sales' and some of the borrowers ran into difficulty because of financial or marketing inexperience. Nevertheless, only three publishers failed to repay their loans and had to be rescued by the guarantee. The scheme was significant in assisting the indigenization of Heinemann Kenya which now, as East African Educational Publishers Limited, is one of the strongest publishing houses on the continent. The project showed that small publishers who are able to gain access to commercial credit and who manage their finances carefully can succeed, even with interest rates as high as 30 to 40 per cent.

Major funders generally were more interested in institutional development than in supplying learning materials. They believed that direct support to pupils and teachers would be less efficient than funding central units for teacher training, curriculum development and educational planning that could increase the effectiveness of the entire system. Books and instructional materials received only a small percentage of total donor aid to education.

Major textbook projects, moreover, were directed to short-term gains to overcome immediate and urgent shortages. Typically, they lasted three to five years and gave little attention to building local publishing capacity. The size, urgency and complexity of the projects precluded local publishers from participating. That responsibility devolved on ministries and parastatals which were themselves ill-prepared and which, outside the project's funding, were at the mercy of legislative budget allocations and government policy changes. There was no long-term approach, among funders or governments, to the sustainable provision of learning materials.

There was, however, a growing interest in co-operation among donors and funding agencies. They met together, formally or informally, to discuss possible joint projects or to exchange information. Some donors preferred that these meetings be held only at the invitation of, and with full participation by, the potential recipients of aid; others were satisfied to meet as a donor group and offer a package of assistance. Some recipients saw the second approach as unfair 'ganging up' on recipients. Donors for African Education, which had been started during the 1980s as a donors' club to promote collaboration in educational projects and programmes in Africa, and thereby avoid competition and duplication, eventually expanded its membership in response to such concerns and, to emphasize partnership over assistance, changed its name to the Association for the Development of Education in Africa (ADEA). Its Working Group on Books and Learning Materials, established in 1989, included African ministries of education as well as development agencies concerned with book development and procurement.

Global trends

The provision of learning materials has been affected, like so many other sectors of society, by the political and economic changes of the decade since Jomtien. Worldwide, the principal trends were towards decentralization of selection and procurement, economic liberalization with a greater role for the private sector and cost recovery to achieve systemic sustainability. The first two trends marched hand in hand, although the balance between them could vary: the state might still dominate in a nominally privatized economy and commercial publishers might be active under centralized state procurement. The third trend, the drive for sustainability, was both a response to budgetary shortfalls in a period of rising demands and rising costs, and a recognition that learning materials are a recurrent expense that cannot practically be financed by continual infusions of external loans and grants.

Change was not always welcomed or rapid. As the authors of a World Bank review observed:

> In all countries entrenched ways of operating and vested interests will make change difficult. Education is intensely political: it affects the majority of citizens, involves all levels of government, almost always makes up the single largest component of public spending in developing countries and involves public subsidies that are biased in favour of the elite. Prevailing systems of education spending and management often protect the interests of teachers' unions, university students, elites, and the central government rather than those of parents, communities, and the poor.

Decentralization

The trend towards decentralization in education had two motivations. One was the democratic belief that all stakeholders should be involved in a function so important to the community' that the wishes of teachers, parents, students, parent-teacher groups and non-governmental organizations should be heard and that some of these groups might be involved in decision-making. In its ultimate expression, responsibility would lodge in the schools, which would be able to decide for themselves how to use substantial portions of their allotted resources, sometimes with the advice of ad hoc committees of teachers, parents, and/or students. The second motivation in many countries was the growing recognition that the existing system didn't work, and one reason was the cost and inertia of swollen bureaucracies.

In the Philippines, for example, a Congressional Commission on Education complained that the Department of Education was 'highly centralized . . . and its complex procedures in asset management have resulted in loss and waste.' It recommended that many responsibilities, including the procurement and distribution of textbooks and other essential materials, be devolved to the country's 126 divisional offices, bypassing entirely the 14 regional offices that lay between the divisions and Manila. Brickhill and Priestley found that 'as a general principle, the further the decision-making process is from the actual user of the material, the less efficiently the funds are used.'

For one reason or the other, governments decentralized the procurement of textbooks and/or their selection if there was a choice. The Russian Federation delegated responsibility for educational funding to the country's oblasts (provinces) in the early 1990s and gave teachers freedom of choice in textbooks. In the economically advanced post-communist countries of Eastern Europe as well, schools or local boards were given their own budgets and allowed to choose their own textbooks. The United Republic of Tanzania announced a policy in 1991 that would lead to selection at the district level and eventually in the schools.

Mexico was to have completed decentralization by the end of 1997, at which time each of the thirty-two provinces would be in control of its schools, teachers and budgets. Colombia devolved selection to the districts and schools, as did Kenya, Uganda, Zimbabwe and some provinces of South Africa. By the end of the decade, India had almost completed devolving the publication of textbooks, teachers' guides and work books to the state governments, which were expected to produce books at a more affordable price than the private sector had been able to achieve.

Not all governments by any means followed the trend or followed it all the way. In Singapore, for example, textbooks were published commercially but the writing of them remained with the Curriculum Development Institute. In Mexico, the government devolved administrative responsibility but not choice; it was reluctant to abandon the idea of 'a single textbook, written and produced by an official body, because it has long been the means of conveying the government's desired message to the population and . . . the record of national history'. In Bangladesh, the National Curriculum and Textbook Board (NCTB) continued to develop the curriculum, write the textbooks and produce the finished books, which it sold at a profit to the Directorate of Primary Education. NCTB opposed any change to the system and, despite proposals by a consortium of funding agencies, the government also showed little active interest in reform.

Decentralization is seen to have several advantages. It encourages the involvement of parents and others in the community. It may give teachers more responsibility and status and, especially in large schools, develop their sense of collegiality. Most important, decisions can be taken in the light of local conditions and to meet local needs. They are no longer made by bureaucrats in a central office, divorced from the realities of the underfunded, often isolated, classroom. Local decision-making is particularly important for rural communities and for minority groups whose concerns, needs, and beliefs have often been ignored in educational books published in' and with examples from' large urban centres.

The transition is not without difficulties, however. Financial decentralization raises concern about money lost through incompetence, misappropriation or corruption. Administratively, there may be confusion if the division of responsibilities is not clearly spelled out. There are often delays in the transfer of funds from the central to subordinate offices. Personnel at all the levels that are given new responsibilities, down to the school, require training in financial accounting, management of supplies, selection of books and other administrative tasks' a massive task. In a strongly hierarchical system, teachers and others are apt to be influenced in their decisions by superior officers, undermining the intent of decentralization. If procurement as well as selection of textbooks is decentralized, retail outlets may not be easily accessible or may be late in obtaining the books for school use.

Liberalization

At the same time as they were moving responsibilities downwards, national governments were withdrawing from the business of providing textbooks and other learning materials. Government departments that wrote and produced text-books as monopolies were turned into parastatal organizations and monopoly publishing parastatals were sold, in part or all, to private owners. Commercial publishers were allowed to compete for textbook adoptions, against one another and, not infrequently, against a parastatal. State-owned printing plants were turned into parastatals and expected to run on strictly commercial lines; parastatal printers were privatized.

The government often retained distribution of school books but, especially in the more liberalized economies, this function too might be given to the publishers. Liberalization was implemented in many patterns, but always in the expectation that commercially oriented enterprises would be more efficient than government and more responsive to educational needs, especially if there were competition in a multi-textbook system. Donors and governments had come to recognize that state monopolies rarely met the need for learning materials and that large-scale subsidies did nothing to encourage reinvestment in publishing development.

In some countries, including Zimbabwe and Jamaica, learning materials had long been supplied by commercial publishers. In others that had had communist governments, commercial production and competition were new concepts to an entire generation. The transition could be abrupt. In the Philippines, a group of commercial textbook publishers and agents, who had been supplying the 5 per cent of the student population in private schools, lobbied the Congress successfully in 1995 to achieve privatization of supply to the much larger and more scattered public system. The state was to get out of textbook writing, production and distribution entirely within three years. The time allowed was inadequate, particularly when implementation was delayed by government inaction and arguments between the public and private sectors, and numerous abuses of the new system in its first year were reported. Other countries approached the transition more cautiously and many were still in the early stages at the decade's end.

The United Republic of Tanzania was one that took a deliberate approach. In 1991 it adopted a policy of transforming the state-managed provision of textbooks into a completely commercial system with minimal government involvement and decentralized selection. A Pilot Project for Publishing (PPP) was established with external support to advise and assist publishers and ministries on an orderly transition. The change was not without its difficulties, but by 1997 commercial publishers had produced 21 titles (1.75 million books) and another 28 titles were in progress.

The first manuscripts were written in the The United Republic of Tanzania Institute of Education, but in 1996 the Institute was restricted to curriculum-related activities. The Ministry of Education continued to be responsible for procurement and distribution. The duration of the transition period has not been defined and will depend on how fast the actors can cope with new responsibilities, and some commercial publishers and booksellers feel the government should move faster in devolving spending power so as to allow full competition.

The beneficial effects of liberalization were to be seen in several countries. In Kenya, which already had a well established publishing industry with significant local ownership, schools were allowed to select the books they would use from up to six titles authorized for each subject/level by the Textbook Approvals Board. The new policies had resulted by 1997 in from three to five competing series in each of five primary-level subjects and comparable choice in subjects at the secondary level except in physics, chemistry and biology, for which books were mainly imported from the United Kingdom.

In other countries progress was slow' outstandingly so in Ghana, where the government had entered into an agreement (heralded as a 'unique, first-of-its-kind effort in all Africa') with five local publishers to co-publish thirty selected primary-school textbooks in 1984 but did not implement it until 1990. It was only three years later that the national publishers' association met for the first time with the Minister of Education to ask for more involvement. Since then the syllabuses, once restricted, have become more publicly available and in 1998 Ghana announced a more open textbook production after consultation with funding agencies, publishers, printers, booksellers, writers and teachers.

In Mongolia, the transition has been hampered by attitudes. The country has experienced and skilled people working in book production, but the business aspects of publishing are not fully understood, and publishers and printers are still primarily looking for funding and not for business opportunities.

Of seventeen countries of sub-Saharan Africa surveyed in 1997, eight apparently continued to use the single textbook system in the publishing of primary-school materials.

One, however, allowed a choice between state-published and privately published titles in some subjects, and three were in transition towards open markets and liberalized textbook publishing. Three countries offered a choice of parallel titles in every subject. Five countries gave limited opportunities for alternative titles in some subjects but not all. There was greater choice at the secondary level. Only Ethiopia and Mozambique apparently restricted schools to single textbooks; other countries had either parallel or, the majority, multiple choice.

At the end of 1998, however, relatively entrepreneurial Cameroon moved away from multiple choice. It signed an agreement granting a newly privatized company, CEPER, S.A., the exclusive right to conceive, produce and distribute all primary and nursery school textbooks in the country. It also exempted CEPER from all taxes on machines, spare parts, paper and ink. CEPER is the successor to the state-owned Centre d'edition et de production pour l'enseignment et recherche which had specialized in educational materials but shared the market with commercial companies, including the well-established Editions CLE. For the most part, the state kept some functions and turned others over to the private sector. In Zambia, manuscripts prepared under the Curriculum Development Institute were tendered to the private sector; the finished books were still being bought centrally in 1996 but there were plans to delegate that responsibility to school management boards. In Lebanon also, a state institution wrote the textbooks, which were then produced and distributed by private publishers. Several Eastern European countries have retained distribution as a governmental function, even though books may be produced in a free market. Occasionally the government has reclaimed responsibilities: Jamaica, which had previously allowed individual secondary schools to order books from their supplier of choice, is moving towards centralization of procurement in order to reduce costs.

In small countries, and in those with languages spoken by only a small population, a continuing state presence was inevitable. Commercial publishers cannot be expected to mount a sales force in countries as small as Niue, which has two schools, or Tokelau, which has three. In those Pacific island countries, central procurement remains the only feasible option. Mauritania encouraged private-sector involvement in publishing but the market was so unattractively small, as a result of population size and poverty, that the state was obliged to write, print and distribute textbooks; even an attempt to involve commercial booksellers in distribution failed. In other small nations, state involvement was by choice. Guyana, with a population of roughly 800,000 and English as a language of instruction, might have used some textbooks produced commercially elsewhere but instead secured external support to write and produce its own primary- and secondary-level textbooks in a government centre.

Where state-owned or parastatal organizations had been forced give up monopoly positions, they frequently continued to dominate the market. As Brickhill has noted, it is difficult to break up a monopoly and establish a level playing field when books are needed immediately and not in two or three years or more. The former monopolists benefited moreover from the conservatism of procurement officers and teachers who hesitated to stray from the former official textbooks. Some parastatals, while autonomous and commercial, still received government funding or hidden benefits such as the use of state-subsidized printing plants. The new publishers did not always prosper. Following liberalization in Kazakhstan, 150 private publishers registered for business in competition with 14 state-owned publishers, but soon after only 12 had survived and only 5 or 6 were effectively functioning.

Funding

In a time of rising enrolments and financial austerity, no

developing country was allocating more than 1 per cent of its primary education budget to textbooks, even though an increase of only 1 or 2 per cent in most countries would have ensured a textbook:pupil ratio of 1:1. Public recurrent expenditures in education were swallowed by teachers' salaries. In a survey of sub-Saharan Africa, only a handful of countries reported what proportion of recurrent educational expenditure was spent on learning materials in 1995 or 1996, but those statistics are gloomy. In primary education, only Mali, at 14.9 per cent, was shown as devoting more than one-tenth of annual recurrent educational expenditures to learning materials; from there the proportion dropped to 8.4 per cent in Comoros, 5.1 per cent in Gambia,1.7 per cent in Seychelles and so on down to 0.2 per cent in Uganda. The reported statistics for secondary education were somewhat higher: from 28.3 per cent to Mali and 8.5 per cent in Togo down to 2.4 per cent in Gambia and 1.4 per cent in Mauritania. Ministries of education were apt to find their legislative masters allocating only a portion of the budget that had been requested to meet stated objectives of free or subsidized text-book provision.

In Indonesia, the books needed to achieve a textbook-to-student ratio of 1:1 in Grades 1 to 9 would have cost an estimated US$380 million in 1995, when the economy was still buoyant; the amount actually spent amounted to US$36 million budgeted by the government and about US$43 million paid by parents' a shortfall of almost 80 per cent (ADEA/UNESCO survey 1999). One respondent with widespread experience observed that the shortage of textbooks is not so much a book famine as a money famine: there are many good quality textbooks available in most subjects in many countries but no funds to buy them and classrooms are generally short of everything but students. Governments admittedly must make difficult choices. Another respondent, this time from the Philippines, recalled that the chair of a congressional committee asked publishers appearing before it: 'How can we even think of books when people are hungry and dying"

In countries that were moving from state or parastatal publishing to private-sector publishing of textbooks, there could be uncomfortable surprises. In principle private enterprise is more efficient than government and should be able to produce text-books more cheaply. But privately owned publishers must recover from sales all their overhead costs' most significantly, wages, premises, office expenses, manuscript development, marketing and interest charges on loans' as well as the costs of production and a reasonable return to shareholders. Ministries that were engaged in publishing normally included only production costs and perhaps some wages in calculating the cost of school books, but they did not always account for those expenses in full and sometimes enjoyed the privilege of state-subsidized printing or tax-exempt paper. Parastatals did not always pay full market costs either. In asking for budgetary allocations, ministries and parastatals used their own calculations to project the annual cost to the government of learning materials.

Those that sold books also often simply charged only the production cost. In contrast, commercial publishers who enjoyed none of the hidden subsidies usually multiplied the cost of production (paper, printing and binding) by three or more to set a retail price that would give them a profit and allow a markup for booksellers. The markup for booksellers could be waived for central procurement by the government, but the price per copy was still likely to be more than double what the Ministry had been accustomed to allowing in its budget estimates. The fiscal allocation would then have to be doubled or more to maintain the same level of provision. If the legislature rejected that option, the number of books that could be bought by the state would be reduced by half or more. Savings could be realized only if the transition to the private sector were accompanied by the appropriate reduction in the civil service establishment, including any senior staff who were writing textbooks or managing publication.

Despite financial stringency, some countries continued to provide textbooks without charge, even if in reduced numbers. Sri Lanka, Nepal, Bhutan and Bangladesh, for example, all provided free textbooks to primary schools, and respondents to the ADEA/ UNESCO survey from those countries reported no book shortages. In countries where an international funding agency was subsidizing textbooks for specific areas (for example, the poorest provinces) or specific groups (girls or indigenous minorities), free distribution was sometimes maintained generally because it was felt inappropriate, if not illegal, to provide textbooks to the rest of the country under less advantageous conditions. It seems likely that free provision will gradually grow less common.

Bhutan is gradually withdrawing support for textbooks and stationery from the economically better-off areas because of rising costs. The Cambodian government is considering selling books for Grade 10 (basic education ends with Grade 9) and may legitimize the sale of core textbooks in lower grades to undermine the black market. Bulgaria suddenly accelerated the introduction of total cost recovery from parents after a World Bank-funded programme ended; what had previously been regarded as politically unacceptable and unaf-fordable suddenly became policy from economic necessity. In the short and medium term, however, governments continue to bear most of the burden of supplying books.

Where textbooks are produced commercially and sold on the open market, there should, of course, be full cost recovery with enough profit to encourage reinvestment in further manuscript development and revision. If necessary, the government may subsidize the publishers.

Where books are not sold, there has been growing attention to at least partial cost recovery through textbook rental. Book banks of this type were established at all levels of education, from primary to tertiary.

There is some evidence that parents prize education so highly as a long-term investment in the family that household demand for education is relatively price-inelastic. That is, enrolment does not drop in proportion to increases in private costs. On the other hand, the elimination of school fees in Uganda led to an increase in enrolment of more than 2 million students. In Samoa, parents grumble at paying school fees of 3 to 5 tala per term, less than the cost of one packet of cigarettes there, and schools, which have difficulty collecting that amount, hesitate to charge more (UNESCO/Danida case-studies: Samoa). Unquestionably, when textbooks are added to the direct costs of education' which may also include exercise books, pencils, uniforms and transportation, even when the schooling itself is free' children from the poorest families are going to be discouraged from attending. In many countries, girls are more likely to be affected than boys, for a variety of reasons: a cultural belief that girls do not need as much schooling as boys because they will spend their lives in domestic tasks, dependence on girls to help with household chores and, the extra cost of clothing for girls.

To compensate, various demand-side support programmes have been devised to encourage attendance by girls, including free textbooks and stipends that can be paid to parents to compensate them for direct costs and for the loss of their daughters' time. Such projects have been undertaken, for example, in Bangladesh, Egypt, Guatemala, Mali, Morocco, Peru, Tunisia and Yemen.

In the Pakistani state of Balochistan, funding for the purchase of textbooks has been part of a rural programme based on community support for schools. In Armenia, where schools operate book rental schemes with a four-year amortization, funds were provided for subsidies to the neediest 10 per cent of students, identified by the school community. A similar scheme has been under way in Guinea

There the book rental fee of approximately US$1.40 per year can be waived if, in the opinion of the school management committee, a student cannot afford to pay it. Funding agencies have also targeted their subsidies to education by directing loans to the most disadvantaged areas of the recipient country. World Bank projects of this kind include support of primary-level textbook development and publishing in six provinces and autonomous regions of China and in ten states of Mexico, both involving the development and publishing of textbooks and other learning materials in indigenous languages that had previously been underserved.

In private schools, textbooks have always been bought by students or families at market rates. The number of private schools varies from country to country and probably reflects to some degree the perception of the public system and the quality of its education. They sometimes play a prominent role. In the Dominican Republic, they have served about 20 per cent of all primary students and 30 per cent of lower-secondary students. In Colombia, private secondary schools outnumbered public ones almost two to one in the eighty-seven municipalities covered by a World Bank project. Private schools normally were located in urban centres and catered to the elite or at least well-to-do. In the second half of the 1990s, the World Bank and other funding agencies began financing projects to increase access to the private system. One method was to issue vouchers for tuition and incidental expenses to needy students. Another was direct funding of private schools serving poor children, as in the Dominican Republic, or serving primary-age girls, as in the Northwest Frontier Province of Pakistan.

Table 1. Projected in enrolment worldwide (in millions)

	1992	*2000*	*Increase (%)*
Primary	522	589	13
Secondary	227	269	19
Post-secondary	32	40	25

Availability of school books

Despite public statements and funders' support, and advances in some countries, it does not appear that textbooks are much more available globally ten years after the World Declaration on Education for All than they were before. Quantitative evidence is scarce, but qualitative reports suggest that, if anything, the situation in many countries has got worse. School enrolments have risen, a result of the demographic curve and national attempts to achieve universal primary education. The number of students attending school worldwide increased by some 50 million between 1990 and 1995, and some 60 million additional children were expected to enter the primary school age group during the next five years. The projected enrolment increases spread across the three educational levels (Table 1) and were expected to be sharpest in sub-Saharan Africa, the Arab States and Southern Asia. At the same time, funding for education has declined as a result of economic slowdown, the cost of servicing foreign debt, devaluation, policies of structural adjustment and competing social needs. Following the collapse of communism, education systems in Eastern Europe and Western Asia have fallen into disarray. In countries with large populations and a history of external textbook support, such as the Philippines and Bangladesh, the international banks are restricting educational loans to the most disadvantaged areas, leaving the majority of the school population to the vagaries of national legislative funding.

In a survey that covered 26 countries of Africa, all but 9 of 103 respondents considered that the book famine in their country was serious, and 87 per cent said there was a serious shortage of textbooks. Respondents to the same questionnaire elsewhere reported serious shortages of textbooks in some grades in Cambodia, for the new curriculum in Mongolia, and more generally in Afghanistan, Indonesia, Lebanon, Pakistan and the

Philippines. There was not total unanimity, however. The respondents from Lebanon and Pakistan differed among themselves, half saying there was in fact no shortage of textbooks.

Such differences of opinion underline the difficulty of judging availability when reliable data are scarce. J. Oliveira said that: Of the 93 countries responding to UNESCO inquiries on the topic, roughly 60 per cent of them (about 57 countries) report that they have a sufficient supply of books; however, several of this group, including Paraguay, Burkina Faso, and Colombia, in fact suffer from a major scarcity of textbooks. This finding not only illustrates that data are not reliable; it also shows that different countries have different opinions about what amount of textbook coverage is sufficient.

Moreover, the numbers given above usually only refer to delivery of textbooks to warehouses, not to what is actually available in school-houses in dense urban periphery neighbourhoods or remote rural villages. According to these same figures, twelve countries report that less than 30 per cent of their schools are supplied with textbooks. In addition, there is extensive evidence that the data regarding textbook use supplied by these and by many other countries are unreliable. Data from other sources . . . are hardly more reliable, since ultimately, they came from the same informants who supplied UNESCO with their education statistics: the Ministries of Education. Askerud concluded that during the last twenty years the ratios of books per pupil had fallen in most developing countries and that for the majority of the world's pupils and students, access to basic tools of learning is so limited as to constitute a major crisis.

A pilot survey of schooling conditions in fourteen of the least developed countries of Africa and Asia, conducted by UNESCO and UNICEF, found that half the pupils had no textbooks.

The survey paints a dismal picture of how classrooms are equipped, making it difficult to imagine how learning can take place. Rural schools generally fare worse than urban ones for learning materials. Final grades tend to be better equipped than the early ones, although conditions are far from adequate. The study found that half of the children have no textbooks. In none of the countries surveyed does every classroom have a usable chalkboard. Very few countries have a world map. No country has all classrooms equipped with a teacher chair and table. Not all children have something with which to write. Ten out of the 14 countries had virtually no supplementary readers, and most countries have no classroom library. These findings give a picture of the gap between official requirements and the actual situation. Most countries have a ministerial norm that there should be one chalkboard, a teacher's chair and a table in each classroom, but these norms were rarely met by more than a small number of schools.

There were pockets of advance, or at least stasis. In Cambodia, for example, the situation improved as a result of external support for the production and free distribution of textbooks for Grades 1 to 9 in the four core subjects: Khmer language, mathematics, science and social studies. Books for Grades 10 to 12 were also being developed and produced in a five-year project. Textbook:pupil ratios were gradually increasing to the target of 1:1 throughout the basic grades. In

Mozambique, too, it was possible for every primary school pupil to have his or her own books as a result of a World Bank loan and subsidies from the Netherlands and Sweden. It was uncertain, however, whether that situation would continue. In an isolated barangay of the central Philippines, 7 km from the nearest town, reached by an unpaved narrow road over hills, visitors to a two-room multi-grade school found an adequate supply of books for the different grades, although they were old and worn. In Egypt, the Ministry of Education gave students one textbook and one activity book each year to keep, reprinting each year to meet new demand.

Kazakhstan almost tripled its annual expenditure on textbooks between 1996 and 1999. As a result, 83 per cent of children in Grade 1 and 70 per cent of children in Grade 2 are reported to have been supplied with a new generation of textbooks that follow post-communist child-centred methods of education. Samplings suggest comparable provision at some other grades. In some areas rural schools are better supplied than urban ones. Textbooks are provided on payment of an annual rental fee from Grades 1 to 9, except for the Grade 1 alphabet book, which is free. The rental fees average about 3 per cent of a monthly family budget, and are waived for needy families. Students in Grade 10 and 11 must buy their books. There is a plan to sell textbooks in the future through the retail market, but needy families would still obtain them without charge.

A survey of six sub-Saharan African countries produced what appear to be favourable relations between target and actual textbook:pupil ratios but the authors describe the data as dubious, because there were rarely any statistics or systematic recording of the situation in schools; they suggest that the most reliable number is that from Zimbabwe, where all textbooks are published commercially and the Ministry has no vested interest in estimating distribution. At mid-decade, spending on education in most sub-Saharan countries had regressed and the shortage of textbooks was said to have reached crisis proportions. In Zambia, the schools had been without sufficient new books for seventeen years. In Ghana, books that had been purchased for the government for free distribution were found in the marketplace, but losses through theft were not unique to that country. In many, textbooks were stolen from government stores or taken from the printers. In Ethiopia, textbooks sometimes reached remote schools before urban schools' an unexpected reversal of the norm' because shipments for the urban schools had been diverted to the black market. UNESCO/Danida case-studies in three African countries also found a continuing shortage of textbooks. In Senegal, the Ministry of Education decided in 1992 to stop the free provision of books and now makes textbooks available to children at comparatively low cost; efforts are made to keep the price lower than commercially produced books.

The textbook:pupil ratio in the schools surveyed ranged from 1:2 to 1:10 for the French reader and from 1:5 to 1:10 for mathematics. Textbooks in science, history and geography were only negligibly available. In general, girls had fewer books than boys. In the United Republic of Tanzania, book shortages were reported in all subjects in the schools surveyed. Books were given free, lent by the school or bought from shops that might be 50 km or more from the school. Schools received books at varying times, most often after the beginning of the school year.

In two urban schools, a text-book: pupil ratio of 1:1 was reported in mathematics, science and English, but in another school there were no Grade 1 text-books. In Grade 4, the ratios ranged from 1:1 to 1:20. Some schools had no books in the national languages. Books were most scarce in the rural schools. Guinea introduced a book rental scheme in 1997, after an unsatisfactory experiment with private- sector provision. Rental schemes are administered by local five-member committees. The distribution of books is not always timely and some of the books are inappropriate for the pupils concerned. Many parents, moreover, are reluctant to rent textbooks for their children because they do not want to incur the possible cost of replacing any that are lost or damaged. Of textbooks that are available in the four core subjects, only a fraction were found to be actually in use. In one school, for example, only 39 per cent of the available textbooks in French were rented, 44 per cent in science, 41 per cent in mathematics and 26 per cent in civic education.

Table 2. Number of subjects and textbook-to-pupil ratios in some sub-Saharan African countries

	Primary education			*Secondary education*		
	No. core subjects	*Text book Planned*	*pupil ratio actual*	*No. core subjects*	*Text book Planned*	*pupil ratio actual*
Botswana	5	1:1	1:1	10	1:1-1:6	1:1-1:6
Ethiopia	4	1:2,1:3	1:2,1:3		1:2-1:3	1:2-1:3
Togo	4	1:1	1:1	5	-	1:10
United Republic of Tanzania	-	1:3	-		1:1	-
Zambia	5	1:2	1:4	5	1:1	1:2
Zimbabwe	5	-	1:7	8	-	-

In Latin America, educational spending emphasized higher education and quality education for a few at the expense of primary education, and especially primary education for the urban poor and the rural population. In the early years of the decade, textbook coverage was reported to average 32 per cent in Chile, Colombia, Bolivia, Ecuador, Panama, Peru and Venezuela. About 76 per cent of pupils in Grades 1 to 3 had one primary or language/art book; about 30 per cent had a mathematics book; and less than 10 per cent had a third book. For Grades 4 and 5 the numbers dropped by 20 per cent. Columbia, Ecuador and Guatemala presented an even bleaker picture. Even middle-income countries such as Brazil, Uruguay and Venezuela had failed to maintain a consistent supply of textbooks. By the end of the decade, however, textbook distribution had improved in some countries at least. In Chile it was universal at both primary and secondary levels as a result of World Bank assistance, successful international competitive bidding and negotiations with publishers in Spain and Mexico as well as Chile. Students had low-cost textbooks, 200 to 300 pages in length, with colour illustrations and good paper, at an average cost of US$3.

In a country as large as India, as might be expected, conditions varied greatly, as exemplified by three UNESCO/Danida case-studies. In a survey of Grades 1 and 5 in nine primary schools in Delhi, the capital, 100 per cent of the pupils were reported as having textbooks, although books were in short supply in one of the schools in Grade 4. Books were supplied free of charge in six schools in lower economic districts, and to 70 per cent of the poorer children in a seventh school. Other children bought their books. Teachers were not provided with textbooks, however, and normally borrowed a copy from a student during classes. In the state of Orissa, in contrast, learning materials were inadequate in all nine of the schools surveyed. Books were supplied free to pupils from Scheduled Castes and Scheduled Tribes, but in quantities well below enrolment. General students bought books on the open market, mostly from teachers who obtained them from outgoing students. Only two of the schools had science kits, and in most schools library books were locked up except during school inspections. Only one of the schools had a lavatory or urinal for children, and only one had even part-year access to safe drinking water. In the state of Maharastra, the State Textbook Bureau provides textbooks, but in practice much of the demand is met by private publishers. Supplies are adequate in urban schools and in schools that are considered average to good. In schools that are considered weak, and in schools in rural areas, there are substantially fewer books. The State policy is to supply books without charge to children in the most disadvantaged groups, but books are provided only to selected classes each year and often arrive more than one month after the beginning of the school year. Illiterate parents often are sold books that are unsuitable for their children's age-group.

In Central Asia, the shortages ranged from significant to critical. Supply was impeded by lack of funding, bureaucratic inertia, inexperience in operating under the post-communist economy, reliance on imports for raw materials and outdated printing equipment. Totally new textbooks were required in the light of revisions of the curriculum to suit new political and social realities and the displacement of Russian as the official language of instruction. In Central and Eastern Europe the situation varied from country to country. In some, new books were scarce and Russian books from before 1990 were still in use. Estimates of the current textbook shortage in the Russian Federation itself begin at 100 million copies and go up from there.

In 1996, the working document prepared for the Mid-Decade Meeting of the International Consultative Forum on Education for All could report that:

> The majority of developing nations have responded to the challenge of the Jomtien Conference by taking various actions to: evaluate their existing education systems; design policies to improve basic education; strengthen the capacities of people and institutions to manage education; create a more supportive policy environment; broaden partnerships and diversify the resource base; and explore ways to use traditional and modern channels of information and communication to provide basic education.

But at the end of the decade, a survey by Oxfam International was less positive in its finding:

> The limited progress towards basic education achieved during the 1990s points to a wide discrepancy between international declarations of intent and substantive planning for change. In the five years after Jomtien, over 100 'education for all' strategies were drawn up by governments, often in co-operation with donors. At the same time, the World Summit for Children, the Social Summit, and the Beijing Conference on Women all generated their own national planning exercises. Some success has been achieved. For instance, the national plans of action drawn up after the World Summit for Children have resulted in major advances in the areas of child and maternal health. In education, by contrast, national planning has generated limited progress. All too often, it has been characterised by vague statements of intent, empty promises, and a

> failure to mobilize resources. A senior official of the World Bank remarked more succinctly that it was 'particularly distressing to see how easy it is for governments to articulate a policy as an objective and not fulfil it'

Quality and use

The quality of textbooks continues to vary. It remains difficult in most countries to find good authors and many books continue to be written by subject specialists or curriculum developers in the Ministry of Education or one of its agencies. Many such authors were still oblivious or indifferent to the experience and abilities of the intended users. A respondent to the ADEA/UNESCO survey described the government-produced textbooks in Pakistan as by and large pedagogically unsound, sometimes filled with mistakes and usually very unattractive, in contrast to the books published by transnationals that are used in the private schools. Another said that student performance in that country in science and social studies is generally low because of the shortage of good books.

In systems with multiple choice of textbooks, there have been complaints, probably inevitable, about the process of evaluation and approval. In Kenya, the government was accused of favouring the former state publishing house. In Romania, officials in the educational system are free to become authors of competing textbooks, leading to concerns about conflict of interest and influence over subordinates. In the Philippines, publishers complained about inconsistency in appraisal: according to one, some books won conditional approval, even though they did not cover all the required curriculum, while others were rejected over an illustration or exercise. During the rapid adoption of new curricula and textbooks after the change of government in South Africa, textbooks, teachers' guides and work books were sometimes evaluated separately and a teachers' guide might be approved while its companion books were rejected.

At the end of the decade, physical quality of textbooks was still poor where printing equipment was outdated and in need of repair, as in Mexico and much of Central Asia, or where paper of good quality was scarce or expensive. Adhesive binding continued to give way and books fell apart. Printed appearance improved in many countries with the spread of computer-assisted composition (also called desktop publishing or DTP) and offset lithographic presses. In replacing traditional forms of typesetting, DTP also speeded the development of new textbooks and the revision of existing ones, although in the hands of undertrained operators it also opened the way to poor typographic design and illustration.

Increasing attention was paid to gender balance, but stereotyping persisted. A science textbook in Pakistan had a page illustrating the functions of various parts of the body: the function of the head, a woman's, was to carry a water pot. A survey in Mozambique, Zambia, and Zimbabwe found that women were under-represented in all the strategic points of textbook publishing and provision' that is, in writing, commissioning, and publishing manuscripts, school procurement and bookshop stocking. In all three countries the authors found evidence in textbooks of gender stereotyping, especially in the portrayal of adults. In Zimbabwe where, unlike the other two countries, textbooks were produced entirely in the private sector, they found 'a continuous thread' of 'gender stereotyping and prejudice against women in virtually any roles outside the home.' Efforts had been made in Zambia at role reversal, role balance and assertiveness of female role models, but stereotyping still appeared in illustrations through order of appearance, role representation, and size, voice and posture.

In the Amman Affirmation adopted by the Mid-Decade Meeting in June 1996, the International Consultative Forum on Education for All acknowledged that progress towards closing the gender gap in education had been excruciatingly slow. It also stressed the essential role of the mother tongue for initial instruction and in that respect, at least, some progress was being made. In Ethiopia, eleven national languages were used in instruction at the national level. In Bolivia, classrooms were allocated books in Quechua, Aymara and Guarini as well as Spanish. In Mexico, an ambitious educational project in ten of the poorest southern states included bilingual textbooks and learning materials for indigenous schools. Textbooks in South Africa are published in eleven official languages. There a large commercial house, Juta, launched an innovative series of learners' resource books, activity books and teachers' resource books in five African languages and were developing them in four more, using stories, folk tales and incidents common to the readers' experience. In the South Pacific, the difficulties of providing learning materials in local languages for small populations was being overcome through regional cooperation.

But the colonial languages have proved tenacious. In the Sahel countries of Burkina Faso, Benin, Niger and Senegal, the state distributed free textbooks in French, bought on a large scale through international competitive bidding, and the national languages were taught only at an experimental level, with no systematic production of materials in them. Indeed, in Burkina Faso there had been a step backwards; the national language was the sole language of instruction until 1985, when the government changed, and only since 1995 has it been gradually reintroduced. Publication in national languages can prove difficult, even controversial, if there is no agreement on orthography. In South Africa, where approval of textbooks is under provincial jurisdiction, a book in Zulu, for example, might be approved in one province and rejected in another because of its spelling.

European experiences and values also persisted. In first grade in Thailand, pupils learned that 'Ama took an apple to school', even though the only apples were expensive imports. In Nepal, 'Sushilla took a bus to the zoo' in fifth grade, although 60 per cent of children living in the mountains had never seen a wheel. In Côte d'Ivoire, primary-school texts were full of French markets and 'my time in Paris'. Such curricula alienated the majority of children from their culture and communities.

There was still no guarantee that teachers would use the books that were available, or use them effectively. Teachers did not always have an accompanying teachers' guide. Sometimes they did not know how to teach when every student had his or her own book; sometimes they were overly protective of the books; sometimes they felt the books provided were not appropriate or relevant to the needs of their pupils. In the increasing number of systems where parents were expected to buy textbooks, some families could not afford the expense, although some countries had programmes to assist their poorest communities. In systems with free distribution, teachers might still be personally responsible for replacing any textbooks that were lost or damaged, and therefore kept them locked up. On the other hand, even when such a policy changed, as in the Philippines, many teachers apparently did not believe that they would not be held responsible for losses or simply were not told of the new directive. Where multiple choice was a new concept after generations of single textbooks, teachers proved unexpectedly resistant to the idea of changing their habits. In Romania, both teachers and parents interpreted the new alternative textbooks as auxiliary to the old 'official' one, and some feared that alternative textbooks would create chaos in the classroom.

Educational materials

In most schools, the textbook and chalkboard were still the primary educational aids. Teachers relied heavily on the textbook, especially in science and mathematics, subjects in which they themselves were apt to be weak. In some jurisdictions, teachers were given lesson plans that they were expected to follow, leaving little scope for creativity or innovation. In the eight countries surveyed in the UNESCO/Danida case-studies, only schools in India and Jamaica reported the availability of electronic aids such as television, tape recorders and computers. All other schools depended on charts, chalk-boards, slates, mathematics sets, books or aids made by the teachers themselves. India began a country-wide programme in 1986 to provide schools with a list of materials, including maps, globes, science kits and flannel boards, but not all the listed materials were received. Classes visited in India under the UNESCO/Danida case-studies were typical of many in developing countries in that:

— teachers read aloud to the class from the textbook;

— teachers asked a few good students to read aloud; teachers asked questions related to what was read aloud, but answered the questions themselves;

— teachers wrote material on the chalkboard for children to copy;

— children copied what was written on the blackboard; and

— children did sums on their slates.

In one class, the teacher was unaware that the children could not find the correct page in their textbook.

In a sample of Jamaican schools, most materials used in the classroom were made by the teachers themselves. Most teachers were trained to use the materials and about 80 per cent of those observed used them appropriately. About three-quarters of the teachers included teaching aids in their lesson plans, and in all but a very few classes the children understood the materials. The materials were more likely to be used if they could be stored in cupboards in the classroom. Most, however, were kept in the head teacher's office.

The use of educational materials was part of pre-service teacher training in all eight countries in the UNESCO case-study survey, but only in Jamaica did teachers feel satisfied that the training was adequate. In Kazakhstan, teachers were receiving intensive training in the use of a new generation of textbooks from teams with expertise in personal and social psychology, educational theory, and curriculum and textbook practices. Authors played a crucial role in the process, visiting schools and demonstrating activities (UNESCO/Danida case-studies:

Kazakhstan). In another country, in contrast, there was no provision for training in the use of educational materials to teach a revised curriculum, the responsibility being left to school inspectors and the Institute of Education.

In some rural schools, pupils were encouraged to collect seeds, grain stalks, match sticks and other items that could be used as teaching aids in mathematics. Children also helped to make aids such as word cards, picture cards, number plates, abacuses, clock faces, balls and pots. Girls generally were more eager to engage in these activities than boys except in Jamaica, where the reverse was true, and in the United Republic of Tanzania, where there was no obvious difference between the genders. In other schools, teaching aids were either completely absent or inadequate in quality and quantity. In some cases they were simply decoration, usually placed above the students' eye level.

A village teacher in Maharastra, India, provided an example of innovative use of low-cost teaching materials. Vaishali Pawar has conscientiously attended in-service training offered to rural teachers in her area by a non-governmental organization. Her classroom has low blackboards on which the pupils can practise handwriting or draw pictures. A few pictorial charts hang at the children's eye level. To supplement reading materials, Vaishali has drawn charts that are large replicas of pages in the Grade 1 language book. Her drawing is not the best, but the charts have child-appeal and she has found that beginners who have problems with the size of the text in their primers are encouraged to read on the big pages. To teach mathematics in her multi-grade class, she uses graded work cards. While she teaches the Grade 1 children, the Grade 2 pupils use the cards individually or in pairs to practise newly learned skills. They thus become actively involved in learning and develop independent study habits.

Some countries were already actively exploring the potential of computers for education early in the 1990s. By 1991, Argentina, Belize, Brazil, Chile, Colombia, Grenada, India, the Republic of Korea, Malaysia, Mexico, Peru, the Philippines, Senegal, Sri Lanka, Swaziland, Thailand, and Trinidad and Tobago had attempted to use computers in at least some schools. India, Mexico and Tunisia were teaching computer literacy at the primary-school level and Argentina, Brazil, Kenya and Senegal were using computers to develop critical thinking, creativity and problem-solving. Costa Rica promised to put computers in half of all primary schools.

Well-designed computer programs had been proven effective: a test in the Philippines found that in 100 hours Grade 1 pupils could learn to read and write English at a level achieved by only a fraction of children in conventional classes at the same school. However, research in North America had already concluded that computers were less cost-effective than other equally effective methods of teaching. In any event, countries that could not afford to provide text-books were hard pressed to find the money for computers or simpler electronic equipment such as videorecorders. And at the end of the decade many' perhaps most' of the schools in Africa and South Asia still lacked reliable electric power to run computers, much less the telephone lines to connect with the Internet. Fewer than 10 per cent of schools in Central Asia had computers. Even in Eastern Europe, where computers were somewhat more common, most were old and could not support CD-ROM or Internet applications.

In a positive contrast, Barbados gave national priority status to installing multimedia facilities in all its schools and was considering including software among the materials available under its well-established textbook rental programme.

Supplementary reading and libraries

In general, supplementary reading materials continued to be scarcer than textbooks. As the decade came to a close, school libraries were said to have the lowest of priorities in educational spending. The majority of schools possessed no library. Where some semblance of a school library did exist, it was often no more than a few shelves of outdated and worn out material, inadequately staffed. A respondent in Bangladesh reported: 'Most of the students do not read books other than prescribed books. The curriculum and learning process in primary education do not encourage students to read or consult books other than the textbooks. There are no libraries attached to the schools or near them'

A study in Samoa found that in nine of the ten schools examined there were few books of any kind, whether instructional or recreational readers, textbooks or teachers' guides. The books that were there tended to be library books donated from overseas (many of them outdated or inappropriate to local culture), instructional readers from New Zealand and a small number of readers produced locally in the early 1990s. It appeared that the few available books were rarely used. Books were found on staff room shelves, in locked cupboards and still in packing boxes. Many were kept in the principal's office and access to them was not easy. Teachers relied instead on the blackboard, charts they had prepared themselves and self-produced books. Children sat on woven mats and read together as the teacher pointed to each word. The rural schools had grid wire windows and on wet, windy days learning material on the walls was ruined.

In southern Africa, better-than-average libraries were usually in secondary schools and heavily reliant on parental support. In Mali, a school library might consist of only 50 to 100 books, including textbooks, in a cupboard in the principal's office; most secondary schools had libraries but lacked suitable premises and budgets for them. In South Africa, the Department of Education and Training, which was responsible for the education of black Africans, did not officially acknowledge the role of school libraries until 1983. In 1997, the Education Foundation found that only 17 per cent of schools in South Africa had libraries and they were concentrated in white and Indian and, to lesser extent coloured, schools. In countries such as Mozambique and Cambodia, schools were destroyed and with them any libraries they had. In Ethiopia, librarians were held directly responsible for any loss of books and were accordingly reluctant to lend them.

School libraries and supplementary reading materials received growing attention during the decade, however. As the post-Jomtien era opened, the World Bank had at least fourteen projects involving primary or secondary school library development and at least five more at the tertiary level. Indonesia had 117,000 school libraries with a total collection of about 106 million books, an average of 900 per school. In the course of the decade small school libraries were centrally procured and distributed in Bolivia, Chile and Peru. In Egypt, a survey of 14 urban and rural schools of varying standards found that students were encouraged to use the school library and learning materials, and most of the schools had a computer and several software programs. The Carnegie Foundation was about to seek opportunities for strengthening libraries in selected African countries.

Cambodia, whose education system had been ravaged by civil war, was developing supplementary materials for the schools, often with support from non-governmental organizations and other international agencies. Up to 100 titles were involved, but some were simply copies of international children's books with Khmer translations pasted in by hand, and distribution tended to be concentrated in core schools in certain provinces. Reference books were almost nonexistent. Two educational magazines aimed at children were fairly widely available in the schools and at bookstalls in Phnom Penh, however, and a few schools had small libraries, especially at the upper secondary level.

A study of African school libraries reported three significant forms of initiative:

> Mali began a 'library in every school' campaign with initial support from the French Co-operation Mission. The pilot project involved 10 schools, with 20 more to follow out of the nearly some 250 public schools that offered nine years of education. For each library, the local community was required to provide appropriate premises, 20 chairs, 2 reading tables, and 2 sets of shelves, and to nominate a teacher to act as librarian. The government would then train the librarian and provide 225 books. Local communities could buy additional books, possibly by raising

money in the cities. The government co-ordinated the network of libraries.

The READ Trust in South Africa, founded in 1979 by a small group of volunteers, had grown to a significant trainer and supplier of materials. The Trust trained teachers in librarianship and in ways to encourage literacy and writing skills. It produced attractive, illustrated books, posters and theme packs designed to dovetail with the curriculum. It put together and distributed classroom libraries of about sixty books' colourful and exciting fiction, non-fiction related to the curriculum and a few reference books such as a dictionary and atlas' stored in a lockable wooden box that doubled as a display cabinet. The libraries could be replenished annually. Students were encouraged to use the books, first in silent reading lessons, then in any free time during school hours, and eventually to take home and share with the family. In reading and writing, children in

READ-equipped classes outperformed control school counterparts by as much as 189 per cent, and were ahead by 18 months in reading scores and two years in writing scores. An average of fifteen boxes per school cost about 20,000 rand (US$4,700), far less than provision of a formal school library.

Box-book libraries were distributed in Mozambique to reinforce understanding of Portuguese, the country's official language but for most people their second one. The project was funded by the Canadian Organization for Development through Education (CODE), but reported to the Cabo Delgado provincial director of the Ministry of Education and was managed by a local non-governmental organization, Progresso. Books bought in

Maputo were sent to the provincial directorate, where they were packed in boxes produced locally and sent to district education officers, who forwarded them to the schools. The initial plan was to create libraries of 150 books (15 titles, each in 10 copies), but by the end 46 titles had been bought, à total of 166,663 volumes. In the first year, all books were imported from Brazil, but locally published books were bought starting in Year 2 and by Year 5 all new purchases were locally produced. Training was incorporated after a midterm evaluation found that many teachers were poorly prepared to teach the early stages of reading and writing. Over five years, about 110,000 pupils were served in 550 schools at a total cost of US$303,117' an average of US$527 per box and US$2.75 per pupil.

In Thailand and the Lao People's Democratic Republic, UNICEF provided more than 400 book-box libraries each year to new graduates of teacher-training colleges and had them carry them to their schools throughout the countries.

Community resource centres' designed to serve an entire community, although often located in schools and used mostly by students and teachers' were appearing in most African countries. The Ghana Book Trust, supported by CODE, bought about US$45,000 worth of books in the mid-1990s, all of them written and published by Ghanaians, and distributed them to community libraries throughout the country. Teachers' resource centres were also established throughout Africa, each of them intended to serve a number of schools with a collection of textbooks, reference materials and classroom sets.

Jamaica was the only country in the UNESCO case-study survey to provide a substantial annual allocation for school libraries and its Library Service is a model for the Caribbean region in its philosophy, structure and systems. The Library Service's mandate includes ensuring that every school has a library. It distributes library books to schools and encourages inter-library loans from the main library to the schools. Schools are encouraged to accept gifts of books but the Library Service assesses whether they are appropriate and up to date. In order to improve school libraries, it runs annual training sessions for principals, teacher/librarians and other staff members. Its effectiveness is constrained, however, by the fact that many schools do not have the room for a library and by the high mobility of professional librarians (UNESCO/Danida case-studies: Jamaica). Commercial publishers, civil society organizations and international agencies took an increasingly active part in the provision of supplementary reading material for children. (Civil society organization is a broad term that includes non-governmental organizations, religious organizations, youth groups, trade unions and other bodies.)

In order to relieve the shortage of children's literature in Kenya, East African Educational Publishers inaugurated a Junior Readers Series in 1988 with 10 books. Ten years later there were 127 titles in the series, some acquired from publishers in other African countries, and with average sales of 3,000 copies the series was the fastest growing section of the publishing house. CODE sponsored a Children's Book Project in the United Republic of Tanzania that assisted the publication of selected titles and bought 3,000 copies of each for distribution to rural libraries and primary schools, with the understanding that the publisher would place at least 2,000 more copies in the open market.

The buy-back ensured that publishers would recover their initial investment, with profit to be made from sales through bookshops. CODE ran a similar, but less ambitious, project in Guyana. In 1997 UNESCO and the African Publishers' Network (APNET) launched a pan-African publishing initiative to produce popular books in science for young adults that would address Africa's energy crisis. Six books are being developed by teams from several countries and will appear in English, French,and Portuguese from local publishers in a series called Science for Africa/KAWI' kawi being Kiswahili for energy. The books will describe alternative energy sources, such as solar energy and biogas, in a context of African experience and folklore, and practical exercises. In Pakistan, the government and donor agencies brought international and local professionals together to produce Urdu fiction and non-fiction books for middle school students. More than 150 titles were produced and placed in 5,000 schools of the Punjab. These and other projects have had to deal with the scarcity of retail book outlets in many countries, and with the reluctance of most booksellers to stock many supplementary readers, which have a less certain sale than textbooks.

Donated books became an important addition to public, school and university libraries. Book Aid International, a British non-governmental organization, sent more half a million books each year to libraries and institutions, responding to profiles of interest submitted by the recipients. It also supported the Inter-African Book Support Scheme, in which selected books from African publishers were bought and sent to African libraries. That programme, and a similar book distribution programme operated by CODE, were found to work best when they were demand-driven' that is, when the books were sent to meet stated needs of the recipients and not as an offloading of unsaleable volumes.

Production of textbooks

Local production of learning materials probably increased during the 1990s, although it is difficult to determine by how much. National interest encouraged the development of local publishing in order to achieve self-reliance, nurture a cultural identity, create local employment and use local printing capacity. On the other hand, the national economy could not always support a local industry, nor could the immediate demands for large numbers of textbooks always be met by national publishers or printers who lacked capital, capacity and experience. At a time of structural adjustment, fiscal stringency, devaluation and inflation in developing countries, foreign publishers had the advantages of sufficient capital, stable currencies and low freight rates. Their branches in developing countries could attract better staff, buy paper and print with the leverage of a large customer, draw for adaptation on the textbooks published by the parent company and sister branches, and benefit from the profit on dictionaries, atlases and other reference works published by the parent organization.

For French publishers in particular, the African textbook market continued to be attractive. Its potential for growth was greater than that of industrialized countries because of demographic curves and efforts to increase net enrolments. Furthermore, the distribution of the world's French-speaking people was shifting away from Europe, towards 50 per cent living in Africa. French publishers invested in African companies, as in Côte d'Ivoire, and the large French publisher Hachette had a subsidiary, EDICEF, specifically to publish textbooks for markets outside France.

British transnationals continued to be active throughout the English-speaking world, although in some places, as in Jamaica, their attempts to establish branches failed and in others they had sold their interests to local publishers, many of whom they had trained. Some British publishers adopted a policy of decentralization, in which autonomous branches operated as regional publishers. Macmillan Kenya, for example, had a local managing director and a fully local staff, published what was appropriate for Kenya without interference from a head office, ran its own in-house training programmes, traded with other African countries regardless of whether they had a Macmillan office of their own, and retained all profits for new projects in Kenya. Macmillan had a more traditional operation in Swaziland, where it assisted in the writing of the textbooks used in the schools and enjoyed a monopoly over their publication. Between 1989 and 1994, British book exports to sub-Saharan Africa increased from just under '39 million to almost'57.5 million. At the end of the decade, however, a British consultant reported that publishers were growing less interested in new initiatives in developing countries because the return on investment was so uncertain.

Book exports were not all from North to South. India, a publishing superstate in its region, was exporting textbooks and other books for children to Southeast Asia and Africa. Malawi met an urgent need for textbooks by inviting publishers from other members of the SADC region to tender titles for it to buy with funding from Danida. The LIMUSA Publishing Company of Mexico published secondary school books for use in Chile, textbooks in primary mathematics for El Salvador, in a variety of subjects for bilingual education in Guatemala, in social science for Nicaragua, and in mathematics and Spanish for Venezuela. Its international success was all the more remarkable in that it was achieved despite state domination of its own domestic text-book market.

Of special importance was a growing tendency towards publishing partnerships between local and non-local firms. Such agreements assumed that textbooks would be sold commercially and envisaged a long-term relationship involving sharing of costs and revenue as well as the transfer of knowledge to the local partner. For example, a Canadian publisher, Irwin, co-operated with Ian Randle Publishers of Jamaica in the development of textbooks for the Caribbean. Another Canadian firm, Fraternité Matin, joined with Jamana in Mali to produce two grammar books. Both partnerships were assisted by a Canadian government initiative, International Publishing Partnership, which provided administrative, informational and financial support. In Cameroon, the French publisher EDICEF worked with a local partner, Editions CLE, to develop textbooks and work books in mathematics and French after the country's externally supported monopoly publisher collapsed. The new books were cheaper than the old ones and were bought by almost 50 per cent of the students in the first year they were available; subsequently the European Union subsidized copies for students in disadvantaged areas.

In what is still a relatively rare example of co-operation between publishers in neighbouring countries,

Fountain Publishers of Uganda was able, with local authors, to adapt text-books in science that had originated with East African Educational Publishers in Kenya. In general, however, regional cross-border trade in educational publishing was impeded by differences in language and syllabuses, trade barriers and difficulties in communication. International agencies played an active part in some joint ventures. UNESCO was involved in a UNDP-funded project to produce a new English course in China. Foreign publishers were invited to tender for the project in co-operation with the People's Education Press, the largest educational publisher in China. The project involved considerable counterpart training. The books continue to be sold, at very low prices, at a rate of more than 40 million copies per year, but the foreign publisher, who was paid a flat fee, barely broke even, making it doubtful whether the venture could be repeated.

Constraints in textbook provision

The constraints that public- and private-sector publishers faced at the end of the decade were little changed from those they faced in 1990, although the increasing role of the private sector and concern about cost recovery resulted in some reconfigurations. Inconsistencies or weaknesses in government were more significant, for example, to private publishers than to a public institution that might be part of the problem. The route towards liberalization had many roadblocks.

Government. Government policy was often inconsistent' not only because of changes in leadership but because of conflicts between government departments. Publishers had to deal with several departments, few of them directly concerned with textbooks. The Ministry of Education normally had the leading role, but the Ministry of Industry might be concerned with protecting domestic printing and manufacture; the Ministry of Trade might be regulating the import and export of paper, machinery and books; the Ministry of Finance possibly regulated the availability of foreign currency, and imposed taxes and tariffs; the Ministry of Agriculture might have some say in the importation of raw materials; and the Ministry of Culture might set language policies, and regulate publishing and printing. Some countries, among them Ghana and Zambia, waived taxes on imported printing goods meant for book publishing, but in other countries local printers and publishers had to pay tax and duties on imported raw materials such as paper at the same time as competitive foreign-produced books were imported duty-free.

More fundamentally, few countries in the developing world had coherent policies for publishing development or the provision of learning materials. Askerud found that lack of funding is often exaggerated as a cause for failure in providing basic learning materials and that other problems are more fundamental. Textbooks did not get the attention they required. Few decision-makers or managers understood publishing or even the difference between publishing and printing, and few gave proper recognition to those in the civil service, or outside it, who did have publishing expertise.

As a result, the design of programmes was left to educators who had little awareness of the professional skills required to produce and distribute quality learning materials successfully, of possible institutional needs for reorganization, staffing and budgeting, of the economics of educational publishing or of the difficulties of marrying educational concerns with the concerns of commercial publishing. From ignorance of the totality and complexity of the book chain, textbooks were treated as simple commodities and planners concentrated only on manuscript development and production. Furthermore, some consultants who had been retained to advise on textbook projects had no interest in seeing local publishing industries develop and ministries were often reluctant to surrender control of textbook provision even when the need was pointed out. Others have also pointed to such problems.

In those countries that were in transition from public to private provision of learning materials, inconsistency and unprofessionalism were apt to be compounded by confusion. Few countries made five- or ten-year plans for the change. Some failed to spell out clearly the roles of the players, the timing of change or the operational details of each phase. The capacity of the private sector was not always taken into account or the need to rebuild publishing skills that had atrophied under state monopoly. If local publishers could not respond to an abrupt transition, the way was opened to foreign ones. In Zambia, for example, the failure of the state monopoly and rapid liberalization led to a renewal of British transnational domination of the market.

Educational statistics remained unreliable and usually outdated. Under such circumstances it was difficult for governments to project requirements or for publishers to determine print runs. Data available from the United Republic of Tanzania indicate the discrepancies in supply and demand that can occur as a result of inadequate information, in this case in a period of increasing private-sector publication and continuing centralized public procurement. Variations of this magnitude can be financially disastrous to commercial publishers. So can unexpected cuts to education budgets by national legislatures. In the Philippines, for example, publishers who had lobbied for privatization were dismayed when they discovered how small the annual funding would be in comparison with the anticipated market. Failures in communication within government further hindered efforts to improve the availability of learning materials. Policies might be communicated so imprecisely that recipients were uncertain what they were expected to do, and as a result did not implement new policies or did so incorrectly. Even clearly-worded policies did not reach the schools, or were not believed when they did arrive. In Mozambique, another kind of failure in communication appeared.

That country had three separate book-box library projects between 1982 and 1996, but there was little exchange of information among them and lessons learned from one project were not transmitted to the next.

Few government officers appreciated the time it takes to write, edit, test and print textbooks. As a result many contracts allowed unrealistically short times from signing to delivery. The resulting textbooks were apt to suffer in quality or would have to be brought in from outside the country.

Political instability, authoritarian governments and war weakened or destroyed both educational and publishing facilities in the most unfortunate countries.

Finance. As devaluation and inflation drove up the cost of imported raw materials, the commercial school book publishers who were being encouraged by the new policies of liberalization and decentralization continued to have great difficulty in finding capital and credit. Investors found publishing unattractive because of low returns and high risk. Banks were reluctant to extend loans because sales revenue in publishing was notoriously unpredictable and few publishers had sufficient collateral or assets. Concessional credit from the World Bank and other international and regional finance institutions, available for agriculture and some other industries, was not extended to book publishing. If loans could be negotiated, interest rates throughout most of the developing world were high' commonly, from 23 to 40 per cent per year. One bank in Ghana did offer loans to publishers but none took up the opportunity because the annual interest rate was 45 per cent. If publishers were able to borrow money at lower rates abroad, they faced the further possible hazard of devaluation. Some in the United Republic of Tanzania went bankrupt after devaluation of the shilling, when the loans they had negotiated in foreign currency had to be repaid.

On a positive note, Nigeria established an Education Trust Fund, analogous to its long-established agricultural development banks, to provide soft loans not only to institutions but to publishers, printers, artists, and others involved in producing learning materials. Payment for textbooks was nearly always slow. Publishers might wait six months or a year for their money, making it even more difficult for them to produce books for the new school year. In Nigeria, the state and federal governments owed publishers considerable amounts of money for books delivered, in some cases, in the previous decade. Governments occasionally discriminated against local publishers, in effect depreciating what capital the publishers had. In Romania, international publishers were invited to bid on text-book provision and guaranteed payment in hard currency.

Local publishers, in contrast, were paid in local currency in the amount established at the time of contract, regardless of any decline in value of the currency by the time books were delivered and payment was finally made. One publisher calculated that his loss from currency instability amounted to 60 per cent in the case of a civics textbook. Joint ventures between local and foreign publishers were discouraged because the foreign partner would receive its share only in local currency. The Ministry of Education further hampered liberalization by establishing unrealistic times for printing and delivery and for teachers to assess competing books.

The capital required to bid on major projects restricted the ability of local companies to participate in major projects funded by the international banks. In Indonesia, private companies were allowed to publish books in a number of fields formerly reserved for the government-owned Balai Pustaka. In practice, only large firms were able to compete. The government issued an invitation in 1999 for bids for textbooks and teachers' guides at the junior secondary level in biology, physics and English. Publishers had to pay 1.5 million rupiahs (about US$220) per subject to obtain the bidding documents. They had further to demonstrate their financial soundness and resources, and prove that they had been operating for at least four years with an important part of their business being the publishing and/or distribution of educational books. This was a year after the collapse of the Indonesian economy and only the biggest of publishers were able to qualify.

In a similar instance two or three years earlier, a West African distributor found it impossible to participate in a World Bank project that involved four textbooks and teachers' guides for the following reasons. It had to find CFA 50,000 (about US$100) to acquire the tender documents, a bank guarantee of 2.5 per cent of the value of the tender and a staff housing tax clearance equal to 1.5 per cent of the salary of each member of the staff. If successful, it would have had to provide CFA 9.8 million (about US$20,000), about 5 per cent of the value of the contract, in guarantees. The company would also have had to demonstrate that it had been financially healthy for some years and had assets worth at least four times the value of the contract sum. The government would advance 30 per cent of the contract price, but only subject to a bank's guarantee. The requirements in this case, coming from both the government and the Bank, effectively doubled the guarantees normally required by the World Bank.

Market size. Not every country was large enough to support a competitive publishing industry. This was evidently true of small island nations, such as those of the Pacific and Caribbean. It was equally true of many other countries. Of the thirty-seven in sub-Saharan Africa, only two or three were thought to have a domestic market large enough to support a book industry, even in primary-level textbooks. In Central and Eastern Europe, the Soros Foundation considered a country in which 7 million people spoke the same language to be a large publishing market, but only ten of the twenty-two former communist countries in which the foundation was active met that criterion. In the other countries print runs and talent pools were smaller and the cost per copy higher. Even the relatively successful book industries of Kenya and Zimbabwe together could draw on a market that was only about one-twentieth of a small European country such as Norway, Denmark or the Netherlands' countries that had a single language and a much better infrastructure.

Local markets were further reduced by photocopying and pirated editions. In most countries, families had limited disposable income for books, including textbooks.

Markets could be expanded by export where there was a common language, as in Latin America. Elsewhere, the barriers mentioned previously worked to restrict publishers to their own countries.

Distribution. It was no easier to reach isolated rural schools at the end of the decade than at its beginning. In the United Republic of Tanzania, for example, official figures in 1994 indicated that more than 16 million textbooks had been delivered to district storerooms over the previous five years. Had all reached the schools, that should have resulted in a textbook:pupil ratio of 1:3 or 1:4. A trial survey that year found that the true ratio was closer to 1:9, with extreme variations between schools and districts. Many books didn't reach the schools, and some that did were kept in school storerooms 'due to uncertainty over supply'. Some books produced by the state were being bought by parents in the market.

Liberalization simply increased the problem if the state was not undertaking responsibility for distribution.

Bookstores were scarce outside the main centres and in many countries even well-established religious or family retail bookstore chains were diversifying, with books as only a minor item. In Latin America, it was said, no publishing house had a distribution network capable of delivering books to every school in every corner of the country, and in many instances books bought by the government simply remained in government warehouses. Kenya sought to resolve the problem by consolidating school orders for textbooks at the district level and then ordering the books from local booksellers, thereby strengthening the retail sector of the book trade and reducing the discrepancies that occurred under central procurement.

Production. Paper remained the principal expense. Some countries, such as Mozambique, had to depend on foreign printing for lack of domestic capacity. In general, the constraints previously noted prevailed.

Human resources. The lack of professionally trained staff continued to hamper state and private publishers in most countries. Large publishing companies did a certain amount of training in-house, however, as did transnationals. In general, the greatest need was in publishing management and marketing, although more training was also needed in textbook development, editing, design and evaluation. A study undertaken by Sida towards the end of the decade drew particular attention to the shortage of well-trained staff at the middle level.

Training received new attention in the 1990s and a number of initiatives were taken. The most ambitious was the African Publishing Institute, a training wing of APNET, which was established in 1992 with the help of several funding agencies, both governmental and non-governmental organizations. The Institute held occasional workshops in its early years. In 1999 it was scheduled to run twenty-two national and regional training workshops throughout the continent, on a variety of topics, and in English, French or Portuguese depending on the country. Workshops are held in co-operation with national publishing associations, using local trainers in accord with a comprehensive syllabus in book publishing and management.

The Asian Cultural Center for UNESCO, supported by the Japanese Ministry of Education and the Japan Book Publishers Association, organized annual courses in various aspects of publishing and book promotion for publishing staff in Asia and Oceania, as it had since 1967. El Centro Regional para el Fomento del Libro en Latina y el Caribe (CERLALC), an international organization created under an agreement between the government of Colombia and UNESCO, offered training courses in book-related topics and published training hand-books for book professionals. UNESCO sponsored training workshops in other countries and, through the International Institute for Educational Planning (IIEP), supported the development and publication of a series of training modules in text-book planning and publishing in Spanish, French, English and Arabic, available in print and for a time as an interactive course on the Internet.

A sampling of other initiatives' and it is only a sampling' illustrates the interest of governments and civil society organizations in publishing training.

The United Kingdom's Department for International Development (DFID, formerly the Overseas Development Administration) sponsored a number of programmes in the Commonwealth and the Arab States. The British Council offered training courses in China, India, Indonesia, Ukraine, the United Republic of Tanzania and Zimbabwe. The Services français pour la coopération bilatéral et multilatérale French Ministry of Co-operation organized training in Africa and France for librarians, publishers, booksellers, authors and illustrators. The Deutsche Stiftung für Internationale Entwicklung (DSE) organized short-and medium-term training courses and workshops in the development of materials, including several concerned with the writing, editing and publishing of textbooks in national languages in French-speaking West Africa. Sida and the Finnish Ministry of Foreign Affairs supported training in Mozambique, the United Republic of Tanzania, and Zambia.

Among non-governmental organizations, the Afro-Asian Book Council organized workshops on author development in Nigeria, Pakistan, Kenya, Ethiopia, and Malaysia. Two German non-governmental organizations offered training internationally, the Deutsche Gesellschaft für Technische Zusammenar-beit (GTZ) and the Ausstellungs und Messe GmbH. The latter turned its training attention from Asia and Africa in the 1990s and ran workshops, with support from the German government, in Central and Eastern Europe. The Centre africain de formation à l'édition et à la diffusion (CAFED), with headquarters in Tunis, offered initial, advanced, and refresher training courses and internships in France for managerial and technical staff.

Coopération par l'éducation et la culture (CEC), a Belgian civil society organization, ran workshops for authors and illustrators of textbooks and children's books in Niger, Tunisia and Zaire. CODE ran training programmes in children's literature, illustration and design in East Africa, and in editing and book design in Guyana. A Norwegian agency, International Movement towards Educational Change (IMTEC), organized a series of workshops on evaluation, editing, illustration and financial controls for textbook publishers of Pakistan. In the 1990s, it organized exchange visits of educational publishers of the Baltic countries and Western Europe. The International Network for the Availability of Scientific Publications (INASP) organized workshops on journal production and management for editors and publishers in Southeast Asia and Africa, and commissioned a reference handbook on book marketing and promotion.

PUBWATCH, a non-governmental organization based in New York, conducted professional workshops, seminars and training schools throughout Central and Eastern Europe and the former Soviet Union, published a quarterly newsletter describing assistance programmes, and sponsored the translation and co-publication of Western guidebooks on book publishing.

The Open Society Institute's Centre for Publishing Development in Budapest created a Web site with material that can be used for training in electronic publishing. The Publishing Training Centre (formerly Book House Training Centre) in London ran courses in Latin America, Central and Southeast Asia, and Central and East Europe, and developed distance learning packages in proofreading, editing and copyright.

Formal education for publishers was also available at universities in a number of countries, although many of the courses were more academic than practical.

Donors and funding agencies

At least 150 agencies' international and regional banks, governments and civil society organizations' had an interest in book development during the 1990s. The breadth of their interest in the development and provision of learning materials is evident in the foregoing pages. Although sustainability was a long-term goal, it was clear, as costs rose and national economies languished, that dependence on external aid would continue for many years. Five trends were significant. Funding. Six years after Jomtiem, the International Consultative Forum on Education for All reported that since 1990 there had been an overall increase in governments' financial commitments and disbursements to basic education. But the decade in general was one of financial belt-tightening in most countries, and as Northern governments reduced their budgets for overseas development, the textbook/learning materials components of educational programmes inevitably were affected. Even so well-established an agency as the Asia/Pacific Cultural Centre for UNESCO announced in 1997 that it would have reduce its activities as a result of the downturn in the Japanese economy. Some bilateral development agencies announced that they would concentrate their activities on a few countries and/or core curriculum subjects.

Non-governmental organizations' local and non-local' had been well represented at Jomtien and were increasingly active, often in innovative ways, in supporting book provision. Many of the non-local ones operated with financial assistance from their governments. CODE, for example, received substantial funding from the Canadian International Development

Agency (CIDA), although the agency itself played little direct part in book provision. Civil society organizations too were affected by global recession, suffering either in government funding or in their fundraising efforts with individuals and corporations. Of particular importance in this context were local civil society organizations associated with the book trade. Among the most important were associations of writers, printers, publishers, booksellers and librarians, who could respond to local conditions and seek common solutions to problems.

Geographic concentration. At the beginning of the decade funding still focused on Africa, the continent most in need of educational assistance. As the educational legacy of communist governments collapsed, attention' from large-scale projects financed by the World Bank and the Asian Development Bank to complementary initiatives by some non-governmental organizations, including the Soros Foundation and PUBWATCH' turned increasingly to countries of East and Central Europe and Central and West Asia. However, the development and provision of textbooks and learning materials, particularly in indigenous languages, continued to be supported by loans and grants in other regions of the world.

Donor co-ordination. From the 1960s to the 1980s, there was little co-ordination among donors: some supported curriculum design, others production, others distribution. During the 1990s there was increasing attention to inter-agency discussion leading to a more coherent approach and an efficient, integrated system for book provision. Towards the end of the decade there was increasing interest in sector-wide support. In this approach, led by Sida, funding agencies meet together with government agencies to work out a plan under which as many parts of the book sector as possible receive the help they need.

The Working Group on Books and Learning Materials of the Association for the Development of Education in Africa (ADEA) provides a forum on book-sector issues for African ministries of education, development agencies and civil society organizations. It encourages the sharing of ideas and experiences among funding agencies, finances research into key areas of book policy; publishes the results of that research and books of practical publishing advice in its series, Perspectives on African Book Development; works with the UNESCO/Danida Initiative on Basic Learning Materials by encouraging collaboration among developing countries in specialized areas of national book development; helps national governments bring together the public and private sectors in book provision; and works with other ADEA working groups to promote education.

The Bellagio Publishing Network is an informal association of donors, African publishers, non-governmental organizations and individuals committed to strengthening indigenous publishing and book development in Africa. The participants meet from time to time to discuss common issues. The Network also publishes a newsletter and a book series that have become an important source of information about publishing development. The group evolved from an international conference on publishing and development organized by the Obor Foundation and held at the Rockefeller Center in Bellagio, Italy, in 1991.

One of the first indirect results of that conference was the formation in 1992 of APNET, which brings together national publishing associations from all sub-Saharan Africa, Enlish-speaking, French-speaking, and Portuguese-speaking. It has been assisted by several government agencies and non-governmental organizations in its work in networking, training, and trade promotion. The Asia-Pacific Cooperative Programme for Reading Promotion and Book Development (APPREB) is a UNESCO-sponsored and supported network of regional institutions and organisations which promote books and reading in Asia and the Pacific region. It was launched in December 1991 in Kuala Lumpur, at UNESCO's initiative, in an attempt to redress the publishing imbalance in the region' one in which many countries have made considerable advances in book development while others remained at an early stage.

The need for further co-ordination remains, however, and conflicts have occasionally arisen between funding agencies. At mid-decade in the Northwest Frontier Province of Pakistan, for example, half a dozen agencies were funding separate projects in curriculum reform and textbook provision. In Cambodia in 1993, an Educational Donors Group had thirty-five members, but about fifteen more operated independently. In Guyana, two funding agencies supported textbook production with DTP technology, with the result that in one room the small nation was learning how to operate separate technologies for primary and secondary level books, one IBM-based, the other Macintosh-based.

In Mozambique, the Netherlands and Swedish governments were supporting Caixa Escolar (the School

Fund), under which consumer subsidies were channeled from the Ministry of Education to district offices for the purchase of textbooks by the schools. The World Bank indicated an interest in the Caixa Escolar scheme in 1993, but eventually funded a parallel system under which books were printed outside the country and distributed free of charge. The Bank's project counteracted the Caixa Escolar system and the newly liberalized Mozambican school policy.

A more fundamental division between funders was in their approach to liberalization. One camp wanted to free production as quickly as possible. The other sought a phased development of capacity. The first was intended to meet immediate needs and often led to involvement, if not dominance, of the market by transnational companies with deep pockets and long-established lists that could be adapted quickly to national needs. The other was intended to provide for an orderly transition and nurture indigenous publishing. Demand-side financing. In the last half of the decade, agencies increasingly rejected the concept of providing printing paper and books as commodities to meet short-term needs for textbooks and learning materials.

More attention was paid to developing a viable system of provision, with concern for all links in the book chain. Sida, for example, decided to change its funding for textbooks, in countries that had begun decentralizing procurement, from the direct support of production processes to support for the development of competence and the local (district or school level) purchase of materials. The World Bank funded a number of educational projects involving demand-side mechanisms such as stipends and vouchers, and targeted subsidies to disadvantaged and minority groups. World Bank policies.

The World Bank was by far the single largest external source of finance for education. Between 1963 and 1997, it was involved in 560 projects in 112 countries, and at the end of that period was still involved in 202 education projects in 88 countries. Its projects ranged from very small countries such as Sao Tome and Principe, with 100,000 people, to China. Between 1980 and 1995, its total volume of lending for education tripled, and education's share in overall Bank lending doubled. Between 1994 and 1997 it lent US$550 million for text-books alone, the greater part for books at the primary level.

Bank funding in 1995 accounted for about one-quarter of all aid to education. Even though that massive assistance represented only about one half of 1 per cent of the total spending in developing countries on education, the Bank's policies were of extraordinary significance. The fact that regional banks marched more or less in step with the World Bank added to the latter's importance.

The World Bank's bank policies were not without critics, in par-ticular its insistence in opening textbooks to international competitive bidding in any contracts above a set threshold. Although the policy was questioned most often in discussions about Africa, in part because of the vigorous advocacy of APNET, that is not the only continent on which the issue has arisen. In the Philippines, international competitive bidding came into open conflict with national law, which required text-books used in the public system to be published by companies that were totally locally owned. The Bank has a general policy of encouraging awards through bidding to the 'lowest evalu-ated bid', a phrase that implies concern for quality and in specific projects has shown some flexibility in implementing competitive bidding' for example, by agreeing to weight bids with price as only a minor factor' but its officers have not been consistent. Regional banks have been somewhat more flexible in requiring international competitive bidding. Despite, or because of, the criticisms, local publishers in both Nigeria and Mali have won competitions for textbooks under World Bank projects against foreign-owned firms.

In 1997, the Bank organized a seminar at which stakeholders from different part of the book chain and from different parts of the world gathered to share their experiences. The proceed-ings of that seminar (Sosale, 1999), frequently quoted in this survey, comprise the most significant published examination of external funding to publishing development since the proceedings of the Bellagio conference at the beginning of the decade.

The seminar itself was part of a policy re-evaluation by the Bank. On the final day, one senior staff member wondered aloud whether the Bank should reconsider its insistence on the 'extraordinarily complex' rules of international competitive bidding for textbooks and look at appropriate national or local competitive bidding or other sorts of supply-side or demand-side financing.

A new Bank policy on textbook provision, released for discussion in draft in 1999, indicates a greater interest in articulating educational publishing with general publishing on the one hand and with educational outcomes on the other. It recognizes the importance of textbooks to a viable publishing industry and the importance of a viable publishing industry to the sustainable provision of learning materials' relationships that will be discussed further in Part V. The Bank's priorities, as set out in the document, are: (a) support to good classroom teaching and learning practice, including a coherent programme for the provision of teachers' guides and teacher training; (b) adherence to legal and other measures for the protection of copyright and other intellectual property rights; (c) articulation of agreed roles of the public and private sectors in the development, production and equitable distribution of textbooks and reading materials; (d) maintenance of transparent and competitive processes in the selection or purchase of books for educational use or for contracting publishing or printing services; and (e) commitment to longer-term financing of book development and provision.

Concerns remain among publishers, nevertheless. The new policy does not address procedural details that were raised at a meeting of West African publishers in 1998. They include high deposits for bidding, inadequate information, complex bidding documents, cumbersome procedures, low advance payments to the winning publisher and delivery periods so short that indigenous publishers cannot hope to meet them.

8

Transforming Technologies in Education

Technology in education has two faces: one of transformation and one of hype. The printing press revolutionized access to education, and in the process an explosion in scientific inquiry was born. Teachers could finally produce and communicate content to a growing number of students entering an industrial revolution.

Classrooms emerged as a great solution to disseminate content and augment interaction with faculty and other students. Traditional apprenticeships with experts polished the student to perfection. Within a short period of time, the industrial workforce ballooned and with it the student body. The need to scale student to teacher interactions encouraged us to turn to other technologies: radio, television, computers, and the World Wide Web. Individually, these technologies couldn't increase the ratio of experts to novices, or significantly add to their real world experience. The "educational transformation" hype emerged around these technologies and they didn't deliver as their evangelists claimed.

Access to computers, especially ones that are connected to communities would have an impact on education. The transformative differentiator for the next generation is the programmability of our interconnected networks. With increases in software programmability, we increase interactivity, increase communication, increase learner adaptability, increase shared visualizations, increase shared laboratory access, and increase experiential learning.

In 20 years, we're going to see an impact equal to the printing press. This time we'll see a global, diverse, educated workforce deliver on dependable innovation, shared vision, and collaborative creativity. The sweet spot for the use of technology in education may clearly be that software personalizes the learning experience, connects all the components, and emancipates publication for targeted and effective interaction.

In the future, no one owns content as an end product. It is molecular at its origin. MIT will give away their content for free, other institutions will follow with interactivity innovations, and quality content will be consumed in chunks by whoever needs it. Through a filter of standards, tools and personalization templates we'll be able to aggregate learning content, the relationships between the content, and our context for using the content in such a way as it becomes part of our own personal value proposition when studying or working with others. The objective: obtain and create knowledge at the right time, in the right place, in the right way, on the right device, for the right person.

Let's imagine where technology will be in 20 years to help us set a vision for taking advantage of this new power for education. Such an exercise will allow us to visualize a roadmap for getting there. From the first few months of life, children play with toys that teach them various concepts. In 2020, toys begin capturing children's learning experiences by using embedded technology that records information about the child's habits, preferences and progress to provide parents with a better understanding of their child's development. Toys provide parents with the child's learning profile, sending private information to the parent's information appliance so they can use the information in the selection and purchase of additional toys that will enhance the child's motivation and experience.

Over the course of the preschool years, children increase their play in Learning 2020 by engaging in supportive virtual reality games in which they build on the psychomotor, reading, writing and math skills they learn in school. Interaction with other students and teachers in the environment helps identify learner strengths and deficiencies.

The environments individualize around the children's content preferences, and create classroom activities that encourage children to expand their abilities through problem solving environments, complete with on- line personalized mentoring by parents and teachers. The games build critical thinking skills using simulated, situational environments that engage other members of the family and community to play along.

Because the parent is more involved, the access to outside content is monitored and manual personalization of student interest can be adjusted accordingly during prescribed home activities as well. The technology objective is to construct a safe environment for the child while engaged in technology driven learning experiences.

For real world interactions, video playbacks of children engaged in learning activities are frequent and reviewed by student, teacher and parent.

Since many parents send their children to kindergarten and traditional K-8 schools, while others home school their children, Learning in 2020 focuses on creating learning environments that facilitate communication and collaboration. Technology networks kids together in groups to learn and practice their combined skills. Whether children are working on art or science, they work with embedded technology that measures their performance.

Capture technologies record student interactions, teacher guidance and parent profiles to provide individualized and group feedback. Continuous personalization ensures each participant brings something unique and cooperative to the group keeping membership optimal. Children communicate with ubiquitous devices that provide targeted feedback to each other while working in groups, identifying compatibilities and suggesting what questions to ask. Group communication is the core objective, with shared activities as the principal methodology.

Students use wearable technologies to exchange, collect, communicate and present information either posted to large screen displays, or holographic 3D environments. As they collect information, it automatically maps to the learning objectives for their skill group and displays cumulative data about the group's success in onscreen graphics for easy monitoring. Anonymity is crucial, as performance indicators supplant grades. The focus on learning is group accomplishment of tasks, with individual contributions sent to the teacher and the student. The environment queries the student when it doesn't receive adequate information and works to help students draw similar inferences that other kids drew during similar exercises. Videos are served up to the students when they don't understand how to do something.

Students complete most of their projects by designing reusable e-books rich with simulations to share their work with others, creating long-term digital portfolios to be shared throughout the years. Teachers help students enhance screen literacy skills by building interactive multimedia for reuse among other learning populations worldwide. Sharing is the key objective, and working in diverse populations is preferred.

Teachers share their activities, thoughts, and technology ideas with a virtual team of experts in business, higher education and other institutions. A strong focus on integrating workflow and student activities throughout the community is enhanced by technology communication systems and easy to use large screen displays that encourage teachers to work together in distances to align industry, institution and schools together in real time knowledge construction and practice.

Teachers are mentors, still using their nurturing techniques in the learning spaces to socialize children. In addition, each child has their own virtual mentor that can be accessed anytime. The mentor follows the children's activities on- line, suggesting new ideas and dialoguing interactively to understand the student's emotions and competencies. When children go on-line, the experience is secure and private. On-line content is filtered by the virtual mentor, who constantly reports noteworthy events to the parents, teachers and other interested parties. Embedded assessment is constantly sent to the teacher, parent and mentor. The virtual mentor consistently maps to performance goals and adjusts student activities to keep kids more focused on learning rather than relying on test taking. Parents can participate in their children's activities wherever they are via wireless mobile video computing and emerging communication technologies.

Learning in 2020 combines the student personalization with the virtual mentor and sends the information out to coordinated work projects designed for community learning. Secured broadband video conferencing appears on every device, digital cameras capture visual content, workspaces grow more complex, and collaboration tools are linked directly to personalized digital libraries. These libraries stay with a learner for life. Digital highlighting, digital conversations, group note-taking and other personal annotations make the asset active throughout the individual's life and can be shared with colleagues at any time.

Since students are working more often in distributed groups, they need to be able to get information more effectively. Students work in groups and ask questions aloud, receiving information through earpieces that feed constant information and personalized entertainment upon request.

As the students work on an experiment trying to figure out how electromagnetism works, for example, they talk through their devices to ask for definitions of words, or ask for a simulation to show them how something like Faraday's law works. Sometimes explanations don't work, so calling up a simulation can help them grasp a concept better. Once they think they understand, they apply the principle to the design and ask for feedback from teachers and co-workers.

Teachers can listen into conversations as well, and they control input when necessary for group messaging or for helping students stay on task. Centralized visualized displays are constantly updated to project student progress, tasks to be performed, and provide guided instructions for learning more about a topic and to help with task completion. Experts are available on-line to evaluate the engineering quality of the students' projects. They are also available to students when they are presenting results, so they can help them deliver their results more effectively. If students are buying materials for their products, the transactions are integrated into their digital financial records, approved by the appropriate person and delivered to the laboratories immediately.

Voice recognition is the standard method of both input and output, occurring mostly outside the classroom where students spend much more time. Students work in laboratories communicating with devices that record student interactions, record hypothesis, previous student engagements, and direct communication links to communities that specialize in the use of the equipment and in the history of effective construction.

Underlying the user's experience is a ubiquitous interface that launches content based on what the student is working on. The interface is a 3D visual bar that can be visually refined to map to the user's experience. For example, if a student begins studying Computer Science, the visual bar identifies his learning objective, his location, his tools, his co-workers, his relevant e- mails, his notifications, the videos, related lectures and text, the experiments, the simulations, the top 10 reading lists, the polls, and the alerts for participating class members. Underneath, likes an assessment tool that reminds the students where to focus attention.

Students work in sophisticated visual environments deconstructing and constructing objects on the screen allowing them to question why things work the way they do. Imagine students using intelligent reusable visual components to build a plane that flies, a bridge that spans a ravine, or an electronic device that can actually be built by another team. As students work in simulated environments with smart learning objects, they begin to understand the underlying scientific principles, and each principle is measured and displayed to allow students to know where they are and what they need to work on next. Force feedback devices provide input that simulates real world instrumentation. Students develop a reason to learn math, and they enhance their communication skills by documenting and annotating their work for review by others.

As students work in collaborative environments, the learning objects adapt immediately to their learning styles in 2020. The tools model the user throughout their learning career. It maps their preexisting knowledge to the kinds of learning objects that are useful to them for rapid learning, much like the toys they used as preschoolers. Now, in this stage of their learning careers, their emotional responses are being tracked to help the m refine their ability to interact even more effectively with others. So many automated processes have been built in for them: inquiry style, learning style, personalized activity selection, multimedia preferences, physical requirements, and favorite hardware devices. For example, if the student is in research mode, natural dialogue inquiry and social filtering tools configure a working environment for asking questions and validating hypotheses. If students like rich multimedia and are working in astronomy, they automatically connected to the Sky Server which accesses all the telescopic pictures of the stars, introduces an on-line expert talking about the individual constellations, and pulls up a chatting environment with other students who are looking at the same environment.

If the student is struggling with a concept, the intelligent tutoring services turn on automatically. If the student needs to practice a psychomotor skill or is restricted because of physical limitations, hardware devices are immediately recommended to assist the student, and locations at various schools nearby are identified for the student to use the equipment. If the student is having difficulty with complex processes or principles either assisted or augmented reality is initiated and the student jumps into a virtual world scenario that gives them an enhanced perspective of the problem and allows them to play the actor solving problems. This is especially useful in engineering and scientific solutions because they also reveal the math behind the phenomena, giving the student real world examples, with the theoretical supporting math. Discovering the visualizations of math can be highly contagious.

The goal of technology, and especially information technology, must be to create an environment where every learner will have a series of resources and teachers in different discipline expertise and in different locations, with a teacher/mentor to help organize the information, and help the student pursue some areas in depth. This is currently too expensive, but there is hope that several upcoming technologies listed below can be deployed in the future. The motivation of the learner is the most important factor in learning. Hence the question becomes - how can technology help and facilitate motivation during the process of learning? We do not advocate replacing the human teacher with the technology!

Future technology must live in a symbiotic relationship amongst teachers, students, parents and society at large. We view the technology as an enabler in a number of ways:

1. Help organize and provide structure for the teacher's material to students
2. Help students, teachers and parents interact, in order to follow progress of learning in a given subject
3. Facilitate and assist in the authentication, search and prioritization of the digital material available on the web, which in this case serves as a world wide encyclopedia
4. Simulate and visualize structures and processes which are the result of physical, chemical, biological and engineering models and to interact in real time with them
5. Help in learning history, and /or future trends because technology can reconstruct life and, hence facilitate visualization of going back and forth in time.
6. A tool for the handicapped population. Technology can serve as an extension and enhancer for their missing capabilities, being either perceptual, physical or cognitive, so that they can equally receive the delivered information for a given subject, just as the

normal population. Several examples might be, for the visually impaired, one can have brail lettered terminals and input/output devices.

For paraplegic subjects there are several robotic customized devices for interacting with teaching material. For the cognitively impaired population, the teaching material must be adapted properly. Here the software enabler mentioned in example1 will be of use This technology can be of great help among the multilingual population, with automated translators available both to teachers, students and parents.

The above enablers depend mostly on subjects which are sufficiently conceptualized and can be delivered through media, such as television or computer screens. Here the information is textual, verbal or pictorial. However, there are skills to be learned that require physical interaction with the world, and/or carrying out an experiment. Here again, the ideal situation would be for each student to have their own experimental setup. However, in many cases this is not possible for a variety of reasons, not the least of which is the cost involved.

In order to have access to expensive laboratories and facilities, one can deploy tele -robotic technologies. With these tele -robots, students can interact with the physical experiment. They can see, hear and feel the affects of the interaction and ask "what if " questions. These kinds of interactions not only help students to understand and embody the knowledge, but it also keeps student's engagement active, which helps them to be motivated.

The most advanced and most desirable technology is the creation of a tele -immersive environment for teaching and learning. This is a three dimensional virtual space, which mimics the real space both visually, aurally and tactually. It is one in which both the student/ apprentice and teacher/master can meet and interact. This technology does not exist yet but it is very feasible from what we know today. The advantages of such an environment are many. First, the students and teachers do not have to be physically collocated. Secondly, the teacher can advise/coach several students and yet the student would feel that he/she is the only one getting the teacher's full attention.

This technology would facilitate demonstration/ coaching of physical and/or mechanical skills (such as surgery, operating complex machinery, etc.), which require true spatio-temporal observations of the master. In turn the master can make the same spatio-temporal observations of the students and give not only verbal but also mechanical feedback. This feedback is critical for the apprentice since it will give him/her a sense of being in direct touch with reality, of being able to control events and get the perceptual feedback concerning how he/she is doing. Finally, we can speculate on multi-site tele - immersive environments which may be needed for the teaching and training of cooperative activities, such as playing in an orchestra, dancing in an ensemble, coordinated war games, coordinated manufacturing and their like. It is not too difficult to extrapolate the one teacher/student scenario to multi-students and one director scenario by deploying the distributed tele-immersive environments.

All of this technology will never be used unless there is sustained and substantial investment into the necessary infrastructure covering not only schools, but libraries and homes, similar to the investment that was made in the past in electrification and later in telephone infrastructure. It is no more amazing now than electricity or the telephone was for us at the very beginning of the third millennium.

The very notion of Internet is disappearing for you because a world without it is simply unthinkable." "Most certainly, but what sort of challenges did you face as an educator in earlier days and how were they overcome?" asks the young teacher. "At the time," continues the veteran, "hardware and awkward user interfaces seemed the formidable foes. "Broadband access to information, wired or wireless, for the consuming public, was neither reliable nor affordable.

Once technological and political barriers were broken, machinery and access costs dropped and the flood of information began to rush in. The challenge was, and remains today, designing technical solutions that, however wondrous, contain a sustainable, scalable economic model and encompass easily used interfaces to access all the features of this rich information environment. Now, about two thirds of the world's eight billion people have anytime, anywhere, anyhow access at an affordable price.

For about 2 billion people today, the Internet is not a reality; it is yet a distant dream or perhaps entirely unknown. Electricity is still unknown or unavailable or unreliable. Sanitation, housing, food, water and education are in limited supply.

For those parts of our global society, Internet and its benefits seem far beyond reach. We must not give up pursuit, however idealistic, of access for all. "Running closely with these challenges was the whole notion of the proper training and use of content.

Learning how to use technology turned out to be at least as challenging as building it. The first computers and online access arrived in the old style classroom back in the mid 1990's. We were all entranced: teachers, administrators, parents. In a decade or two, three complementary interfaces will shape how people learn:

— The familiar "world to the desk top" interface, providing access to distant experts and archives, enabling collaborations, mentoring relationships, and virtual communities-of-practice. This interface is evolving through initiatives such as Internet.

— Interfaces for "ubiquitous computing," in which portable wireless devices infuse virtual resources as we move through the real world. The early stages of "augmented reality" interfaces are characterized by research on the role of "smart objects" and "intelligent contexts" in learning and doing.

— "Alice-in-Wonderland" multi-user virtual environments interfaces, in which participants' avatars interact with computer-based agents and digital artifacts in virtual contexts. The initial stages of studies on shared virtual environments are characterized by advances in Internet games and work in virtual reality.

The important issue in effectiveness for learning is not the sophistication of the technologies, but the ways in which their capabilities aid and motivate users.

Life Long Learning

Computing has already enriched and enhanced people's lives in countless ways, but we've only begun to see how it will transform our businesses, our governments and our communities. In the next few years - in the "digital decade" - we'll see computing become a much more significant and indispensable part of all our lives.

The pace of innovation is accelerating in all the core technologies of computing - from processing power to storage to network bandwidth - making it possible for computers to become better connected, easier and more intuitive to use, even less costly, and capable of handling all kinds of information. While this will create countless opportunities for business, entertainment and communication, the application of these technologies to the way people learn is the most important - and exciting.

By giving students access to a new world of information, sparking creativity, and facilitating rich communication and collaboration across vast distances, computers have long been a powerful tool for education. At the same time, the Internet has brought an unprecedented level of great educational content to a wide audience, encouraging teachers to share curriculums and resources worldwide.

E- mail has facilitated improved communication among administrators, teachers, students, parents and educational researchers, and emerging Web services technologies will create further opportunities for collaborative learning. Increased industry and government funding in learning science promises to vastly improve the ways technology is applied to learning.

In the years ahead, a whole generation of kids will leave college and enter the workforce with a broad understanding of the ways they can use technology effectively in their jobs. But we've still got a long way to go before we see how much technology can really do - particularly in education. Solving business problems with computers looks easy when compared to the often complex and little-understood process of learning. And technology is only part of the solution. All the computers in the world won't make a difference without enthusiastic students, skilled and committed teachers, involved and informed parents, and a society that underscores the value of lifelong learning. Finding effective ways to use technology to enhance learning is a challenge that educators, academics, policymakers and the technology industry must work together to solve.

Simulation Technologies

Simulation technologies and powerful sensor technologies provide scaleable models for engaging in the learning by doing. Simulations allow students the opportunity to build integrated environments with objects in one environment that serve similar purposes in another environment. This level of programmability across multiple visual environments is the metric for successful development. As students move from the visual world to the real world, sensors in laboratories provide students with feedback as they reconstruct and deconstruct various objects in real time, with real materials.

Intelligent Laboratory Objects

Embedded technology now designs learning into any object used in education. Students receive physical components that instruct the student how to design, test, and connect them together. Students build robots frequently to perform various functions to prove their concepts. If the student fails to create a solution, he automatically remediates to a visual environment for practice and better visualization of key concepts. If the student still struggles with the content and actions, he is sent back to the original set of instruction and exercises through an on- line video conferencing environment. Internet based laboratories are the norm where students are able to run laboratory experiments wherever they find them, meaning that not all schools don't have to budget to build exactly the same capabilities. Instrumentation is managed remotely and students work together in laboratory groups to learn how to use equipment effectively.

Project Management

Students write more software in 2020, not least because all scientific disciplines require increasing amounts of computing sophistication. So, they must be taught to identify opportunities and customers, manage their requirements, provide effective documentation, and manage source code, release management, testing and usability. Students manage several projects with outside customers through internet interfaces, virtual conferences, and shared workspaces. Task analysis software is personalized and everyone who is responsible for an action item is automatically notified, as well as all the related collaborators.

Voice technology eases communication as students wear technology in their clothing allowing them to access both content and people wherever they are. Students are finally getting a grip on how to program software, teach programming to their coworkers or team members, and manage software projects.

Paying games to learn complex skills

The military medic and the civilian Emergency Medical Technician (EMT) must be prepared to perform difficult, life-saving procedures, often in the face of traumatic injury and danger. These challenges have been increased with the emergence of Weapons of Mass Destruction (WMD), and the realization that civilian healthcare personnel in the United States may have to cope with mass casualties requiring prompt and effective medical care under difficult environmental conditions.

Like playing a musical instrument or flying a plane, medical procedures involve both cognitive and technical skills that demand frequent rehearsal for proper execution. Treating a patient in crisis with the added burden imposed by dangerous settings such as the combat battlefield may produce a stressful experience for the medic, sometimes leading to faulty decisions and medical errors. Unfortunately, skills such as Cardiopulmonary Resuscitation (CPR) are easily forgotten, and there is little opportunity for medics and other healthcare personnel to refresh their skills through practice on real patients in settings that approximate the dangers of the battlefield or the mass casualty event.

Computer-based simulation has been used extensively in the airline industry and in the military for effective training of cognitive, perceptual and motor skills. More recently, simulators have been used for training medical personnel in procedures using manikins and virtual reality systems.

Medical simulators may include both three-dimensional (3D) models of human anatomy displayed on a computer monitor coupled with a "haptics" device that conveys a sense of touch to the user. Thus, a paramedic inserting a chest tube or a surgeon cutting into a 'virtual' patient can visualize anatomy and feel the forces associated with the actual procedure using a force feedback device similar to the controllers used in computer gaming.

In addition to the value provided by simulators for skill training, these systems can also provide an ongoing assessment of the performance of the trainee, including metrics such as judgment, timing, sequencing of procedural steps, spatial accuracy, errors, etc. In medicine, the development of performance metrics and the objective assessment of performance is a difficult and complex process, because it requires decomposing the medical procedures into their elemental parts using a process called task analysis, depends on 'buy-in' from experts in the medical community, and requires validation using rigorous scientific methods. The performance can be displayed to the user in a debriefing session, and compared to the user's past performance and to the performance of other users. When properly configured and validated, computer-based simulators can provide objective assessment of performance to be used for certification in medicine, as they have been used for certification in aviation.

One approach for refreshing and sustaining technical skills is to allow the medic and other healthcare personnel to practice procedures in simulated environments that reproduce many of the difficulties found in real world, emergency settings. An advantage offered by simulation in all domains is the ability to expose personnel to unusual settings and situations where practice improves performance and reduces error in real world tasks.

The ideal medic training system would provide refresher training both in the field and at dedicated training centers, be deployable on a variety of hardware platforms, ranging from PDAs and laptops to full-blown immersive virtual reality training systems, be networked into larger simulations such as wargames and into hospital information systems to provide updated medical information, allow for retrieval of the user's past performance in relevant patient cases including replay of video, and be available for testing and skills certification.

However, in the short term, an optimal simulation game for medic training should at the very least, encompass the latest in learning technologies within the constraints imposed by medical training. The goal is to embed skills, judgment and knowledge so deeply into the central nervous system of the medic that diagnosis and therapy are promptly and effectively executed for point-of-wounding care even in the most dire and stressful of circumstances.

Patient case-based scenarios are a common tool for differential diagnosis and therapy in medicine. Providing the medic with a choice of case studies, retrieved by user input or automatically as part of the learning process, greatly enhances the training value of the simulation. Thus, if the simulation determines that that the student is having trouble placing an intravenous line, additional cases are called up from the database for training in venous access. In some cases, the trainee should be able to successfully perform the medical procedure by any number of alternate, valid pathways. This is often critical in medicine, since many procedures can be successfully performed using different approaches, many of which may arise as a consequence of the specific complications, anatomical anomalies, or combination of procedural elements that are

1. Automated patient case scenario retrieval based on the location, training need and circumstances as indicated by the user, or generated from the software program, including automated reach back functionality to select appropriate cases for training;
2. Recording of student state for on-the-fly adjustment of training resources;
3. Intelligent tutoring that can track the performance of each individual's progress during instruction and encourage trainees to formulate questions when they're confused, providing context -sensitive answers when appropriate, and summon human instructors when needed;
4. Performance assessment based metrics validated by the medical community, resulting in automated debriefing providing interpretation of cognitive skills and technical skills as part of the After Action Review (AAR).
5. Scalable training with SCORM (Shareable Courseware Object Reference Model)-compliant content modules, including different versions for field and training center applications;
6. Competitive and engaging computer graphics-based game environments, allowing trainees to compete

against each other and expert users, including single player and career modes, in the context of appropriate combat settings including specific ground warfare sites;

7. Distributed, networked capabilities supporting multi-player including team training capabilities and allowing interface with other systems;
8. Learning Management System, including event recorder and common administration database containing user performance ratings; Support for hardware interfaces and functionalities, including compatibility with laptop delivery platform, video capabilities for student state recording and playback modes, and extensions to immersive virtual reality devices presented by the specific patient case. The simulation should not only be able to track the student's progress through the content, it should also be able to determine the cognitive and emotional state of the student, determined by how the user behavior in the simulation, or by more direct physiologic measures of the student state such as EMG or video analysis, and adapt the instructional content to suit the needs of the trainee. Intelligent tutors, programmed into the simulation, or available as live experts accessible online, should provide remedial help when needed. Automated debriefing can list and score the correct and incorrect choices, for review by the trainee and his/her superiors.

Although great progress is being made in the development of computer simulation for skills training, the next generation of medical simulators will greatly extend the benefits of this approach through advances in technology. Today, we can envision the value of simulation training by providing medics with the opportunity to refresh their skills with engaging gameplay and validated medical content. In the next few years, not only will visually realistic simulators run on the desktop, they will also support sophisticated functions such as the integration of physiology to create realistic "breathing and bleeding" human simulations, predictive human models that can integrate diagnostic image data and laboratory tests to forecast disease within specific patients, simulations that can serve as testbeds for new therapies, drugs and interventions, and simulated surrogates that substitute for actual humans in dangerous settings.

The eventual goal of research and development efforts will be the development of a coordinated "Digital Human", consisting of models, simulations and databases spanning molecule to organism. The challenge posed by this work is that a valid and accurate model of human structure and function can be built to serve as the standard for medical diagnostics, therapeutics and education.

Given an aggressive investment and skillful management, technologies achievable by the year 2020 could transform learning - making it more productive, more personalized and more compelling for learners of any age and with any background. These technologies will make it possible to implement a range of powerful new instructional strategies long recommended by experts in cognition, but which were previously unaffordable. The instructional strategies enabled by these new technologies will more closely resemble some of the earliest forms of instruction based on tutors and apprenticeships than today's factory-like classrooms. For example, new tools will permit learners to explore and test their skills in simulated environments unaffordable or unattainable in any previous learning system. These new learning systems will change the process of learning, redefine the role played by the teachers, and create an enormous range of challenging new teaching occupations. What they will not do is replace the need for human teachers, tutors and counselors who can provide expert instruction, provide inspiration, encouragement and discipline, and serve as exemplars of the kinds of expertise a learner can aspire to achieve. Teaching and other related occupations in education and training systems will become much more like other "knowledge economy" professions, having more opportunities for professional growth and more support from technology and specialists.

In many sectors of economy, skillful use of technology has resulted in an increase in the quality of products and services, greater personalization of services, increased efficiency and reduced costs. Realizing these benefits required coupling information technology with careful rethinking of the processes, management structures and job descriptions of the people and institutions involved. There is no reason to believe that education will be any different. Consider what has happened in medicine. As little as a generation ago the occupations in medicine were largely limited to family doctors and nurses. But today, modern physicians can draw on an enormous array of medical professionals to provide specialized expertise, develop and maintain sophisticated medical equipment and software, and perform elaborate testing. It would be down right frightening if your medical care was limited to what your family physician could perform in his office - but that is largely the situation teachers find themselves in today.

By the year 2020, teachers will routinely work with teams of people with expertise in many different areas and draw upon a variety of learning products and services. New learning systems will enable teachers to create challenging assignments that can close the gap between the world of instruction and the world of work and tailor instruction to increase the efficiency of learning. New learning systems will make more productive use of both the teacher's and learner's time and talents and provide useful, multi-dimensional assessments of each learner's expertise and ability to accomplish complex tasks. For example:

· The process of learning will dramatically extend from "teacher push" to "learner pull." With future learning systems, human instructors and a robust array of software tools will shape the instructional path in ways that can be most efficient and most motivating for each individual. In the right time and place, lectures will still be critical, but current learning environments too often consist of sitting passively in a room with a hundred people and little expectation of being an active participant.

Next generation learning systems will allow learners to access live and recorded lectures from multiple sources. Performance-based assignments will allow learners and small groups to demonstrate levels of expertise in tasks where they are strongly motivated to succeed. Learning systems will be built from a set of powerful tools allowing instructional designers to go from concept to operational systems quickly. They will also permit continuous upgrades and improvements as problems are discovered and new concepts are proposed and tested. The tools will include systems for: continuously evaluating the learner's approach to expertise in critical areas; providing quick, context-sensitive, individualized responses to questions by dispatching questions to automated systems and human tutors and experts; rapidly building networks of learners and teachers; monitoring a user's level of interest, anxiety and motivation; adapting to specific learners (language of instruction, cultural background, learning abilities); and systems for building simulations reflecting the state-of-the-art in science, engineering and other fields.

Robust simulations will make possible assignments in which learners learn and test their expertise in addressing compelling assignments and problems. Coursework could include being turned loose in a virtual representation of Renaissance Venice and asked to find the secret behind the legendary blue coloring of their glass, engineering and building a (virtual) bridge over a (virtual) Mississippi River, navigating the interior of a (virtual) pancreatic cell to determine why signals reaching it do not stimulate insulin, or being given a broken (virtual) avionics system from a Boeing 777 and asked to repair it.

Teachers and learners will be able to call on a variety human tutors, counselors and experts and summon a variety of automated help systems for addressing routine questions. Learners will work face-to-face with teachers and tutors and be able to call on a worldwide network of subject-matter experts and other specialists when interesting questions arise. Sophisticated tools will help diagnose sources of confusion and suggest new learning strategies based on analysis of the experience of large numbers of learners facing similar situations.

A combination of automated monitoring tools, tutors and other specialists will make it possible to continuously adjust the pace, nature and style of the learning process to ensure a learning experience optimized for each learner. Instead of being forced to move all learners forward at a uniform rate, teachers will be able to move each individual forward at a rate consistent with his or her measured performance in each area. No one will be forced forward before demonstrating comfort and confidence in the concepts being learned. This combination of automated and human observers will enable continuous measures of competence integral to the learning process that can help teachers work more effectively with individuals and leave a record of competence that is useful and informative to learners, future teachers and employers.

As in every other sector of the economy that learned to make effective use of new information tools, these gains will require dramatic changes in the organizational structures and management systems of the institutions that deliver education and training services. Education and training institutions and their supporting industries must dramatically improve the way they invest in innovation, manage innovation, invest in capital equipment and assign responsibilities to different occupations. These changes will reshape the nature of employment in education in a number of ways:

— Teaching will become much more personalized because teachers will be able to spend much more time in dialogues with individuals and small groups.

— The roles bundled in the job of today's teachers are likely to be "unbundled" (lecturer, tutor, counselor, subject-matter expert, administrator, disciplinarian, record keeper, evaluator, curriculum designer) with many tasks performed by experts or automated systems with specialized expertise.

— As a consequence, teachers and tutors working directly with learners will work as a part of sophisticated and continuously changing team involving specialists and specialty firms. Professionals may specialize as subject-matter experts, expert teachers, instructional designers, courseware developers, applications designers, or a variety of other occupations, and they may concentrate on the roles at which they excel and find most rewarding. Individuals may undertake several roles simultaneously and are likely to move between jobs for career advancement or because an inspired opportunity defines a business opportunity.

— The new supporting industries will generate an enormous number of new occupational opportunities. Many of these will be in firms that produce tools and services sold to a large number of education and training institutions (and in some cases to individuals) worldwide. Since many of the skills involved will be required by other businesses, movement into and out of education professions is likely - a process that will ensure that education takes full value of innovations occurring throughout the economy. Online instruction will make it much easier for individuals to build new skills that would allow individuals to change specialties during the course of their careers.

— Professionals at all levels will need to continuously upgrade their skills and use an array of tools for professional development throughout their careers.

> This can include keeping abreast of developments in the field being taught, understanding advances in the theory of cognition, pedagogy and assessment, and understanding innovations in software design, standards and communications.

Fortunately teachers and other professionals will work in an environment allowing easy access to high quality instruction in all areas-sometimes using tools they themselves have developed. Demonstrations of expert teaching will be readily available over the high-speed internet, and the new information tools can let teachers see discussions on how other teachers have approached a subject or dealt with a difficult situation and facilitate dialogues with their colleagues as they struggle with similar issues.

The improvements in teaching and learning just described will require a major national investment in research and skillful management of these innovations by education and training institutions. The needed research will require large, persistent, well-managed research programs and partnerships drawing on industry, government, foundations, universities and schools.

New learning systems will only be affordable if these research insights are used to build robust, reliable, well-evaluated tools that allow investments to be amortized over a large number of users. It may, for example, cost several million dollars to build a powerful biomedical simulation, but the investment can be returned quickly if the product and interaction model can be used by hundreds of thousands of course designers and teachers worldwide. It may seem expensive to employ specialists in specific types of learning disabilities, but if the specialists can work online to quickly diagnose and advise teachers and learners in a large region the amortized cost will be affordable. Making effective use of these tools and redefining the roles of teachers and other professionals needed to use them to achieve real gains in learning will require creative management by education and training institutions and supporting industries.

The challenging new occupations of teaching, tool building and support services will give education occupations the same respect, and same remuneration, enjoyed by other knowledge professionals. There will be much more room for professional growth and mobility, and more time to learn from colleagues and specialists. Society will need to make a choice about whether the efficiency gains will be used to cut the cost of delivering high quality education and training or whether to use it to deliver more and better education and training services to more people. We suspect that both will happen and that markets and political leaders will recognize that increased investment in professionally delivered learning services is a key to a prosperous and just society.

Future jobs

These jobs may be performed onsite or offsite and the services may be provided by the institution or purchased from other providers Notes Gifted lecturers and experts in various fields capable of giving outstanding and unique presentations that can motivate and inspire Some individuals may be some superstars used widely by teachers and learners Teachers and tutors gifted in working closely with individual learners may work face-to-face with learners or exchanges may be via online exchanges.

Counselors sensitive to the individual needs, interests, abilities, and cultural background of each learner may do site visits but generally will work with learners online

Learning specialists who have specialized expertise in assisting learners with particular learning difficulties and disabilities may do site visits but generally will work with learners online.

Subject-matter experts who define instructional requirements for courses and propose strategies to evaluate whether appropriate expertise has been reached will work with professional societies, certification organizations and employers

Curriculum designers who work as part of a design team to translate objectives into creative courses of instruction.

Competing firms may specialize in instructional modules or entire suites of instruction Simulation and virtual environments engineers who build and maintain the components for synthetic environments, including specialized scientific software, e.g. a digital human that can be used for a variety of learning situations. Specialists in building the components of simulated towns, instruments, landscapes, biological systems, or physical phenomena.

Software engineers who work in teams to develop and maintain systems that can track individual learner progress, help provide accurate automated answers and summon instructors.

Developers of tools for continuous evaluation of a learner's expertise, "user models" of motivation, state of confusion, diagnose confusion and take approximate action.

Evaluation and certification experts who ensure that the knowledge and expertise measured match instructional goals Independent measures of expertise or certification of embedded assessments.

Management and support occupations that provide a variety of services including record keeping, IP management, repair, MIS systems, micropayments, etc. may be provided by the institution or services and software tools may be purchased or licensed from specialty firms.

Classroom Model for 2020

A new paradigm for K-12 education will evolve over the next 20 years as innovative information technology and pedagogy are integrated into the learning environment. This process is being fueled by two factors: broadband Internet capability and the emergence of immersive technologies. When these technologies are combined, the Internet as we know it today will be transformed from a low fidelity medium for browsing information to a high fidelity medium that delivers rich and immersive experiences. These new remote immersion systems will bring interactive and stimulating classroom experiences to all student populations - regardless of location. Classroom boundaries will fade as students and teachers are brought together by high-resolution video and immersive 3D shared environments that allow natural discussion, collaboration, and interaction among physically distant participants.

With remote immersion, students and teachers will investigate, play, explore, and learn together in an environment that dynamically adapts to the content - from a biology laboratory to a visit to the aquarium. The transformation of the Internet into a system for rich experiences will bring about the creation of massive distributed online archives of past lectures, interactive presentations, simulations, proficiency testing, and problem presentations. This new content, designed specifically for these new technologies, will replace current textbooks and workbooks with a national resource of high-production and content quality materials, cross-indexed and customized for individuals or classes. Once created, the archives will be updated and further improved by continuous contributions and links from teachers, production groups, and authors anywhere.

Advances in information management technology will be integrated with both the delivery and content creation technologies to address the critical need for meaningful learning assessment. Rather than relying on current periodic testing results, automated tracking of students' progress will provide statistical models of presentation sequences and paths, providing instant feedback to the student, the instructors, and administrators on progress or problems in the curriculum and its presentation. There is a great need within the education community for such innovations and the pressure to make changes is being felt by schools at all levels. While information and digital media technology has been progressing at breakneck speeds over the past decade, unfortunately little has changed in the delivery and the design of the curriculum.

The majority of efforts involving technology in education have focused on CD-ROMs or web sites containing little more than digitized versions of textbooks, or broadcast lectures with poor quality audio and video. Little has been done to design the content to take advantage of the potential of new delivery mechanisms.

Technology up to now has been viewed as a way of reaching a larger audience, and not as the enabler of new learning paradigms. We envision a new partnership evolving between technology and pedagogy-a partnership that will result in a new education paradigm. Teachers and students might be thousands of miles apart, yet they will appear and sound to each other as if they are in the same classroom.

Facilitated by unobtrusive picture and sound display devices, the infrastructure will give them a strong sense of presence, as if they are actually in the room together. Students will be able to "touch" objects in a faraway museum or "feel" forces in a virtual physics experiment through the use of haptics (touch-based technology).

Teachers will be able to search for past lectures that best suit the needs of the session at this time. Data acquired automatically from the student's interactions in this immersive environment will be captured and used to optimize the lesson progression.

The term interactivity will be transformed from mouse-clicking and instant messaging to realistic, life-sized representations of teachers and classmates sitting next to you and talking. Imagine students interacting with avatars of James Watson and Francis Crick tutoring and guiding them on the discovery of the DNA structure. Imagine students immersed in a role playing experience at the Continental Congress during the Revolutionary War era. This is what remote immersion can do for education. As appealing as this vision may sound, the truly revolutionary transformation will take place at the core-the dramatic reformation of our teaching methods themselves.

New approaches will be developed for content authoring and modeling for simulation and for creating models of learning and assessment to measure the progress of students and guide them through the learning and problem-solving process. Students will interact with content material, explore challenges and perform inquiry-driven collaborative investigations, using an array of virtual laboratory tools and simulations. This new education environment will incorporate 3D computer animation and graphics, real-time image rendering, multichannel immersive audio, video, text, and haptics. Techniques that promote a high degree of student attention, goal attainment motivation, and satisfaction will be adapted from approaches already much better understood and employed by the gaming industry.

New multimedia and Internet technologies are creating novel ways to teach and learn through this very process of creating new ways to see, hear, and touch. From an educational viewpoint, the use of sensory immersion has never been investigated. There is evidence from learning and psychology research indicating that memory is significantly enhanced by spatial associations. For example, optimal recall is achieved when an experience is not only captured as a set of sound and image streams, but when these are reproduced in such a fashion that the replay experience preserves the spatial relationships among the various elements. How will this paradigm of bringing remote teachers and students together improve our standard classroom where the teacher and students are already in one place? It extends the classroom, opening it up to a vast treasure trove of educational experiences beyond the physical room walls and delivered in specific ways designed and crafted to enhance learning and understanding. Clearly, when the teachers and students are physically in the same classroom, the technology will still deliver experiences and materials in a way that enhances learning. This will also open the door to consistent and continued education for children with disabilities, or those in medical institutions, or those with difficulties traveling to a classroom. The new paradigm of K-12 education we envision will evolve steadily over the next decade. As the technologies are introduced, we also envision the transformation of society in countless other ways, including the ways we communicate socially, conduct business, produce goods, and entertain ourselves.

Broad dynamic content will feed future education technologies. We will integrate motion and haptic interfaces, display and sound sciences, computer simulation breakthroughs, and next-level communication and information technologies. The vast possibilities created by these merging technologies make it crucial to bring together great minds from every discipline to begin building a foundation for the development of massive amounts of evolving content simultaneously and in collaboration with the design of next-generation education technology.

Future education process

The future of education will be profoundly affected by forthcoming information technology. But even more importantly, it will be affected by how educators and students use the technology to prepare for lifelong learning in the face of unrelenting change. Human beings have been slowly evolving along with their tools for millennia, but we have now entered an age in which revolutionary transformations take place every few years. This makes it difficult for most people to even imagine what technology will be available in two decades, let alone for institutions to plan its effective use.

Exponential change presents the danger that people will be swept away by an irresistible flood of new technologies that supplant all that they have learned, making them irrelevant to society and incapable of contributing to it. However, in the hands of skillful and dedicated teachers, new information technologies have the potential to greatly improve the educational process. People of any age with access to them may learn to embrace change as an exhilarating part of life and adapt as rapidly as the world about them transforms. The responsibility for determining whether technology overwhelms or elevates future students belongs to everyone, not just the developers and marketers of products. More than ever, the joint efforts of concerned teachers and involved parents will be needed to ensure the proper use of technology in the classroom so that education becomes an integral part of living.

Extrapolating from historical advances in electronics, we can roughly predict some of the tools that will be available in 20 years:

— Hand-held (or wearable) computers will be able to calculate 10,000 times faster than they can today, and will thus begin to rival the data processing capability of the human brain. They will be the hubs of digital assistants that could store more textual information than a human could read in 10 lifetimes. Such assistants will combine the present functions of telephones, web browsers, and recorders and players of both audio and video. Through wireless web access, they will be able to download far more video information than a human could watch in a lifetime.

— Digital assistants may be capable of real conversation, responding to verbal requests with questions to clarify the requester's intent. A third party wouldn't be able to tell if a person is conversing with his or her digital assistant or with another person, using the assistant as a telephone.

— Display technology will also have advanced tremendously. In 20 years, we'll have eyeglass displays that will be able to project virtual or recorded images that the wearer will perceive as immersive three-dimensional reality. Such glasses will be able to overlay or blend telemetry, virtual images and the real world almost seamlessly. A person will be able to see someone seated across a table, and - in the next "seat" - another person physically located halfway around the globe.

If we accept these projections, what can we guess about the future of education and learning? We can imagine two extreme scenarios following from present trends: the first a distinctly bleak but all too possible future and the second a vision in which teachers and technology work together to help students realize their full potential.

A blind acceptance and inexpert use of information technology in future classrooms could lead to a generation of people with no ability to interact with each other or with the unpredictable surprises and accidents that occur in everyday life. Judging from the way in which computers are often used in schools today - by teachers who don't understand technology or are intimidated by it - we can easily envision a future in which teachers in elementary school use immersive technology as digital Ritalin, to keep young students quiet and docile.

The students themselves could become addicted to the virtual worlds they are presented and prefer them to the real world. This scenario projects that children in the future will have very little contact directly with each other and would become social misfits. This is not all that far-fetched, since all too often today young children come home from school to turn on their computers rather than going out to play with each other. It could also mean that tomorrow's students will have too little experience of the real world: if they are given a steady diet of prepared scenarios and virtual models, they will be totally unprepared and unable to deal with new problems that arise. A model can only have built into it the types of behaviors that people understand or have already experienced; however, Murphy is a lot smarter than any programmer, so a student brought up on canned solutions to problems may be completely overwhelmed by a unique experience or interaction.

Furthermore, if education software is an extension of current computer games, then all children will have homogenized backgrounds and will react to the same stimulus in the same fashion. Technology used in this improper fashion has the capacity to crush the creativity out of young people and turn them into obliging responders to prepackaged stimuli, such as advertisements or political propaganda. Does that mean that children under a certain age should be banned from using computers, rather like today's youth are denied cigarettes? That's not a desirable (nor practical) objective, since highly capable computers can and should be used to encourage and enhance the creativity of a person. However, teachers and parents must carefully consider how to introduce and stage students' work with computers as one component of their educational experience. In the optimistic scenario, new technologies properly utilized in the classroom have the potential for encouraging differentiation and creativity.

Very few people have the skill with a brush to craft a great painting or the facility with the musical scales to compose a symphony. But with appropriate technology and software, it should be possible to digitally create any image or sound that a person can imagine. This possibility dramatically expands the range of assignments that young learners can tackle and the ways in which they can express themselves. They key is that the tools are used as an extension to creativity, not a set of fixed restrictions on what a student can do.

Traditional classroom learning involves experiencing new material at least five times: previewing a textbook, listening to a lecture, reading the text for comprehension, performing directed problem solving and reviewing the information (usually for an examination that is intended to gauge how well the student mastered the material). This paradigm can be adapted for highly capable digital assistants, where new material is introduced gradually over a period of time by presenting it within meaningful contexts, the lecture could be a recording of a great master teacher, the reading for comprehension could be done with an active tutor that senses when the learner is having difficulties, etc.

All of this presupposes that real people with a strong sense of social responsibility become involved in creating the software and the environments that are used in the learning experience. This will require that we better comprehend human cognition and use that improved understanding in designing our tools to establish a sound pedagogy. Thus, improved technology provides greater imperatives for performing research in areas that will help us to be more aware of ourselves. The daily experiences of teachers must be incorporated into any new approach to curricula, so that they will work with digital assistants to customize lessons according each pupil's aptitudes and interests.

Above all, we must understand that there can be no substitute for direct human contact, even with all of the imperfections and misunderstandings that can arise. People have always learned best through their mistakes or the mistakes of others, and no technology will change that. Given these considerations - the need to use technology appropriately and not attempt to substitute it for human interaction or experience with the real world - future technology could provide qualitatively new types of learning.

The human aural system is similar to a serial communications channel, which is greatly afflicted by noise and transmission errors. Normal human writing and reading emulates this serial process. However, vision is inherently a parallel information communication system. People with sight can see everything within a two-dimensional frame simultaneously, and, moreover, that frame can be updated frequently. That means learning and comprehension may benefit greatly from the development of a universal visual language. Such a language is in a sense already developing - it appears in a wide variety of media and it is also evolving through viewgraph presentations, where a presenter can mix aural and visual stimuli to convey large amounts of complex information in a short time.

Future book equivalents may actually be written in a visual language, in which more information-rich symbols are used, perhaps something like hieroglyphics as clip art. A U.S. student studying South Africa could not only attend lectures and discussions, read books, listen to music, see the art and cultural artifacts, watch TV and films, and access a wealth of factual information on the Internet, he or she could also meet and communicate in a universal language directly with a South African student studying the U.S. to appreciate different perspectives and world-views.

In short, tomorrow's educational environment should be greatly enhanced by future information technology, which can engage more of the senses in the learning experience for vastly improved comprehension. The ubiquitous availability of information could abolish the constraints of time and place for education, which should become a part of the fabric of everyday life. And everyone should have equal access and be able to contribute to the continual flow of new information, which in turn must be verifiable or subject to review and rebuttal! This approach to education recalls the universal truth attributed to both Chinese and Native American wisdom: "Tell me and I'll forget. Show me and I may remember. Involve me and I'll understand." We must all become involved, not only in understanding future technologies but the ways in which those technologies will be put to use. Technology can never be a substitute for excellent teachers and involved parents, but it can enable a more enriching and effective educational experience for those fortunate enough to be in an environment where it is used properly. The future begins today.

In theory, technology offers endless possibilities to enhance the educational experience. Educational technology can offer students expanded academic opportunities as well as critical employment skills necessary for entering the workforce of the global economy. Technology may have the potential to transform from a goal to a reality the ideal that every child will succeed academically. In practice, however, what we do in the present will define our future. And, as in space travel and medicine, technological advances in education will require major national commitment and resources.

By the next decade, technology could bring students to exciting new worlds, enhance teaching and learning strategies, and facilitate effective parental involvement. Twenty-four hour access and pervasive technology will be the norm. Students will require both technological fluency, and whole new levels of media literacy skills. Educational employees will have a vast array of tools to tap the potential of every child, but will also face the significant challenge of managing these new responsibilities.

Bibliography

Bare, J., and Meek, A. 1998. *Internet Access in Public Schools* (NCES 98-031). U.S. Depart-ment of Education, National Center for Education Statistics. Washington, DC: U.S. Government Printing Office.

Heaviside S., Riggins, T., and Farris, E. 1997. *Advanced Telecommunications in U.S. Public Elementary and Secondary Schools,* Fall 1996 (NCES 97-944). U.S. Department of Education, National Center for Education Statistics. Washington, DC: U.S. Government Printing Office.

Heaviside, S., and Farris, E. 1997. *Advanced Telecommunications in U.S. Private Schools, K-12,* Fall 1995 (NCES 97-394). U.S. Depart-ment of Education, National Center for Education Statistics. Washington, DC: U.S. Government Printing Office.

Heaviside, S., Farris, E., and Malitz, G. 1995. *Advanced Telecommunications in U.S. Public Schools*, K-12 (NCES 95-731). U.S. Depart-ment of Education, National Center for Education Statistics. Washington, DC: U.S.Government Printing Office.

Heaviside, S., Rowand, C., Hurst, D., and McArthur, E. 2000. *What Are the Barriers to the Use of Advanced Telecommunications for Students with Disabilities in Public Schools?* (NCES 2000-042). U.S. Department of Education, National Center for Education Statistics. Washington, DC: U.S. Government Printing Office.

Levin, D., Hurst, D., and Burns, S. 2000. *Computer and Internet Access in U.S. Private Schools and Classrooms: 1995 and 1998*

(NCES 2000-044). U.S. Department of Education, National Center for Education Statistics. Washington, DC: U.S. Government Printing Office.

Lytras, M. D. and G. I. Doukidis (2001). *'E-Learning Pedagogy: Define the Value'. Technology in Education International Conference & Exposition* (TechEd 2001), March 26-29, 2001 Southern California ,USA .

Lytras, M. D. and H. Odman (2001). *Fulfilling organizational learning on concurrent enterprises: The Multidimensional Dynamic Learning model for knowledge management exploitation.* 7th International Conference on Concurrent Enterprising (ICE 2001), June 26-27, 2001, Bremen, Germany.

Riley, R., Holleman, F., and Roberts, L. 2000. *eLearning: Putting a World-Class Education at the Fingertips of All Children.U.S. Department of Education,* Office of Educational Technology. This document is available online (http://www.ed.gov/Technology/elearning/e-learning.pdf).

Rowand, C. 1999. *Internet Access in Public Schools and Classrooms: 1994-98* (NCES 1999-017). U.S. Department of Education, National Center for Education Statistics. Washington, DC: U.S. Government Printing Office.

Ryan, M. (1995). *Human resource management and the politics of knowledge:linking the essential knowledge base of the organization to strategic decision making.* Leadership and Organizational Development Journal Vol. 16(No. 5).

Shuell, T. J. (1992). *Designing instructional computing systems for meaningful learning.* In M. Jones & P. H. Winne (Eds.), Adaptive learning environments: Foundations and frontiers, New York: Springer- Verlag, pp.19-54.

Smerdon, B., Cronen, S., Lanahan, L., Anderson, J., Iannotti, N., and Angeles, J. 2000. *Teachers' Tools for the 21st Century: A Report on Teachers' Use of Technology* (NCES 2000-102). U.S. Department of Education, National Center for Education Statistics. Washington, DC: U.S. Government Printing Office. Williams, C. 2000. Internet Access in Public Schools and Classrooms: 1994-99 (NCES 2000-086). U.S. Department of Education,

Index